The Interesting Tale of
LOGGAM MAGGEL

VALERIE CUNNINGHAM

PAGE PUBLISHING, INC.
Conneaut Lake, PA

First originally published by Page Publishing 2020

ISBN 978-1-64584-259-0 (pbk)
ISBN 978-1-64584-260-6 (digital)

Printed in the United States of America

Dedication

You were my first friend, then my best friend and always my biggest inspiration.

The gratitude I feel in my heart to have you as my mother is unmatched by anything else in this world or beyond.

Thank you for always being my biggest fan and my guiding light. You believed in me even when I sometimes didn't believe in myself. I love you mom.

And to my husband, you'll always be my forever... I love you sweetheart.

Miss you always my sweet Freddy.

Prologue

Red Fir

Most state parks are known for their natural beauty: panoramic landscapes scattered with all sorts of colorful trees, mountains, lakes, lazy rivers, and wildlife. Red Fir Mountain shares all those qualities, but one of its most interesting features is the tale of Loggam Maggel, an interesting name for an interesting character. Loggam lived in a small cottage with his mother on the corner of Red Fir Mountain State Park. The park was his playground, his school, and his social outlet, and it was at this park that Loggam learned how to survive off the land and the kindness of others. In return, he made Red Fir Mountain State Park one of the most widely recognized state parks as well as most popular for visiting.

When Loggam was a young boy, he and his mom walked through the park every morning. The cool breeze, the swaying trees, the leaves, and the familiar crunchy sounds under his feet were one of his favorite things to experience. During their walks, they spoke with campers that came from all over the United States and some even from other countries like Canada and once even a man from Russia. Loggam learned about life through his casual conversations over meals with various campers through the years. He realized the one thing many of the campers liked was a campfire conversation. So every afternoon, he would walk through the woods collecting logs for firewood, and he would offer the firewood to his camper friends in exchange for a meal for him and his mom. Loggam knew Red Fir State Park better than any park ranger in Alabama for he walked those woods every day, sometimes all day. It was his home, and it would be there that his story came alive.

When Loggam was eighteen years old, a camper friend had given him a lottery ticket and a Tootsie pop. The ticket amused him; it was the first one he'd ever had. He had never even seen one up close before and tucked it away in his back pocket and eagerly went to the real treasure, his Tootsie pop. Later that evening, when he arrived home, he scratched off the coating on the ticket, and it revealed that his life would suddenly change—he would now be a multimillionaire. He studied that ticket meticulously wondering what matching these numbers and winning would mean for him and his mom. Hours passed, and yet Loggam still sat there scratching his chin staring at the ticket. Loggam was the first eighteen-year-old man to ever win the multimillion-dollar state lottery. At first, he didn't even know how much he won—he had never seen a number with so many zeros—but soon he would learn that he was about to make the news. He was a simple young man with little desires; he knew all the money in the world wouldn't get him to leave his woods. The campers were always pleased to see him, and although his life was simple, he could share so many stories with his friends because over the years, he learned so many things from the campers in the park. Although he had never moved from Alabama, or even the town where he lived, in his imagination and through the stories that he heard from the travelers, he had traveled the world over and over. He learned about many cultures, tried so many different foods, and he even learned some other languages that the campers spoke. The campers were his teachers and his friends.

One day a few months after Loggam's big win, while he was walking through the park he observed a child jumping up and down with thrill. He wondered, *Why is this child so excited?* And the child ran to his mom and showed her what he had found on the ground— it was a shiny quarter. Loggam found that so amusing because he had so many of those, and he wasn't half as excited about it as that child was. It reminded him of all his treasure hunts for rocks when he was a small child and how excited the mere search to find them was. Then like a lightning bolt, an idea came to him, and he found himself experiencing the same degree of excitement, something he had never felt before. With the biggest smile on his sweet freckled face, he couldn't wait for morning to put his plan into action.

When morning finally came Loggam jumped out of bed and sprang into action. The sun was truly amazing, it was one of those sunrises that was gently obscured by the morning fog, and so with the veil of the fog you could look directly at the awesomeness of the sun and observe how incredible it really was. He used that beautiful morning sunshine to light the path that he would begin on. Loggam visited the bank and got $100 all in change—all kinds of change: silver dollars, fifty-cent pieces, dimes, nickels, and pennies. When he returned to Red Fir, his pockets were full to the brim. The rest of the coins he put in a Ziploc bag.

He walked over to Skully Lake as this area held the thickest population of campers because the firepits and BBQ grills were all set up here. He reached in deep into his pockets and tossed those coins up in the air. He watched as they came down like rain and covered the ground. The ground gleamed as the sun shone against the shiny surfaces of the coins. All the campsites and recreation areas would get a little of this love every day except Sunday. On Sundays, Loggam would spend his time just basking in the joy that he brought to the visitors at the park as they found his treasures across the woody landscape. He'd watch as the children would run through the wooded trees and search through piles of leaves to unearth the glistening coins. When they'd find them, they'd lift each one in the air and cheer before tucking them into their pockets and searching some more. The pleasure he felt watching these children warmed his heart intensely. These precious moments taught him how wonderful it felt to bring joy to others. Loggam knew that it would become his life's mission to help people every chance he could. He knew that he was blessed with such good fortune for a purpose, and it would be his goal to pass it on.

Over the span of many years, Loggam's truest desires to love and help others truly succeeded. He would enrich the lives of more people than he'd even realized. This small-town boy changed the footprint of countless people's lives by having a heart full of love and an insatiable desire to add beauty to the world. Even as a child, Loggam had a beautiful way about him. His positive demeanor and zest for life were unmatched. Friends of Loggam have said he must be magical because of the charisma he possessed. The more he did to help others; it came back to him in the form of many blessings. Some of the accomplishments Loggam had would almost seem impossibly done by this small-town country boy, but with enough heart, anything truly is possible. The only questions that remains is what will he do next?

Part One

A Special Loggam Maggel Christmas

A little boy with shady blond hair, freckles scattered across his cheeks, and his daddy's all-too-big jacket overwhelming his nine-year-old frame, walked outside to collect stones for his massive rock collection. Loggam and his mother, Judith, lived in a small cottage just beside the grounds of Red Fir Mountain State Park. It is where they've been living since Loggam was a newborn baby. His home was those trees, hills, mountains, and lakes, even more so than their cottage. He loved being outdoors regardless of how cold or hot the weather was. Judith watched from the big bay window as Loggam examined each stone he picked up, and with a quick nod, he would put them into his big pockets. He could be at this for hours without rest. When it was dinnertime, Judith called him back inside where they had a stew she made from leftovers in her fridge. Judith didn't have very much money to buy many groceries. Even since her husband had passed away two years earlier, she's done all she can to make ends meet. She picked up a small job when Loggam was in school to keep the lights on.

"Yummy in my tummy!" Loggam exclaimed. He loved his mama's cooking.

"Did you find more stones for your collection, sweetheart?"

"Oh yeah, I got this really shiny one that is my favorite. Want to see it?" Loggam reached in his pockets and pulled out a big shiny black rock. He was so impressed with it, he flipped it around in his hand to show her every ridge, and he had a new favorite.

"Well, you should put that in your display case, Loggam."

"Oh, I am, and it's going to go right in the front. This is a special rock, and I just know it."

After washing the dishes with his mom, Loggam retreated to his small bedroom with hunter green curtains and a bedspread. He went over to his dresser and pulled out a plastic clear box. He removed the few stones inside and put in his newest special find. He then had it perched on the top of his dresser so he could admire his newest treasure.

The next morning, Loggam had a bright idea. Because he loved his rock so much, he decided he would take the pocketknife his dad taught him how to safely use and carve a word into the front flat surface of the rock. Very meticulously he carved the letters *S-P-E-C-I-A-L* into the rock. When the impression was deep enough, he was satisfied and returned it to the display case. This was now his special rock, and whenever he held it, he felt consumed by a happy feeling. Loggam got dressed in blue jeans and his dad's old sweater. It went down to his knees, but he didn't care; he liked that it still carried his scent. He went down for breakfast that his mom had waiting for him. "Good morning, sweetheart. Did you sleep well?"

"I slept great. I think that rock is special, Mama. It gave me dreams of daddy all night. I felt like he was in my room with me."

"Oh, my love, he is always with you, right beside you—that, I promise you."

It made Loggam feel so good hearing that, he just hugged the sweater he wore tight across his little body. Together, they ate their oatmeal and started to discuss Christmas coming soon.

"So, have you written your letter to Santa Claus, Mama?"

"Oh, I will write mine soon, but more importantly, have you written yours, Loggam?"

"Well, not yet… I haven't decided what I want for Christmas yet, and I don't wanna seem wishy-washy with the big guy."

Judith chuckled at that and remarked that she understood. "Hey, Loggam, I noticed over by Skully Lake, new campers have arrived. It looks like they have a little girl around your age. I thought maybe we'd take a walk over and welcome them. Would you like to do that?"

"Absolute-e-tootly!"

Judith and Loggam grabbed their red wagon and started loading up some firewood during the walk over to Skully Lake. By the time they arrived, they had a huge stack ready to go.

A couple stood outside of the camper, just taking in the view.

"Hello there. My name is Judith, and this is my boy, Loggam. we just wanted to welcome you to Red Fir and bring you some firewood."

"Why, thank you very much. It's great to meet you, Judith, and you, Loggam. My name is Ken Mallet and this is my wife, Mindy. We have a little one about your age, too, named Jenny. She's just taking a nap right now, but I'm sure she'd love to meet you both. Are you fellow campers?"

"We actually are not. We live about a mile East towards Briar Circle right outside of the state park. We've lived here for many years, so if you should have any questions, please feel free to ask either of us. Even though Loggam's only nine, I don't think there is anything he doesn't know about these woods!"

Mindy chuckled and decided to invite Judith and Loggam for dinner with them that evening. They kindly accepted the offer and told them they'd come back around 5:00 PM.

After Judith and Loggam left, they gathered more firewood and made their rounds to other campers. Most greeted them as family as they'd made many close friends over the years of living here. Janice Greenblatt stopped them and ran into to camper and came back out with a chocolate cake she made for them.

"Oh, thank you, Janice. That was so sweet of you."

"That cake looks so sweet!" exclaimed Loggam. Both ladies giggled and hugged.

"It was my pleasure; I've been looking out for you two all morning to pass here!" Janice kissed Loggam's cheek and then Judith's and the two of them were off again this time with a chocolate cake in their wagon.

Judith and Loggam arrived back at Ken and Mindy's campsite at 5:00 PM. Ken and Mindy were both already outside, and Mindy had been grilling chicken, which smelled delicious. Loggam offered to help set up a firepit for later that evening. As he gathered some wood, he heard the sound of a little girl speaking. This was the first time Loggam had seen Jenny since they'd arrived. Loggam was a bit confused by her appearance. She wore a bandana around her head where her hair should be and looked skinnier than any other girls his age he'd ever seen. As she walked over to him, he noticed she had very pale skin and dark circles under her eyes. Though he was slightly put off by her appearance, he put out his hand as his parents always taught him and introduced himself to her. Jenny giggled at him and very softly shook his hand back.

"How old are you?" Jenny asked.

"I am nine, how old are you?"

"I am eight," she said.

"Have you ever had a pet?"

"Yeah, I have a cat at home named George, and I had goldfish, but they went to goldfish heaven, my mom said," Jenny replied.

"Wanna see something cool my dad showed me, Jenny?"

"Sure!"

With that, Loggam went over and picked up two sticks he inspected and started rubbing them together. Nothing special was happening, but Jenny was enjoying watching waiting for whatever was supposed to. After a few minutes of furiously trying, Loggam said, "It works sometimes and sometimes it doesn't. When it does though, I can make *fire!*"

"Wow, really that's so cool."

Jenny and Loggam continued talking and getting to know one another while their parents did the same.

After they all finished eating, Loggam asked if they could roast marshmallows and have some hot chocolate. Judith was a bit uneasy because she didn't bring any with her and didn't want to impose on the Mallets. Ken and Mindy were all too pleased to have them stay and indulge in some cocoa; they had more than enough to go around, they said.

As they sat around the fire talking and getting sticky from the marshmallows, Judith asked, "Are you all staying for Christmas?"

"Yes, we are. We thought it would be nice to spend it here in Alabama. We live in Gatlinburg, Tennessee, and though it's beautiful this time of year, we wanted to try a change of scenery," Ken replied.

"Well, that's wonderful. We have many festivities we do for the season. In fact, tomorrow, Loggam and I are gonna go out and cut down our Christmas tree if you'd all like to join us."

"That sounds wonderful," Mindy replied.

The next morning, Loggam was getting all of his dad's Christmas tree cutting gear ready. He had a bow saw, some rope, his red wagon, and gloves. Judith was always so amazed at how well Loggam seemed to recall everything his father did and exactly how he did it. They met with the Mallets, and with all their supplies ready to go as well, set off. Ken took the handle from Loggam and suggested he pull both wagons so Loggam can lead the way.

As they walked further into the woods more and more Leyland cypress trees came into view. They were so beautiful and so many different sizes! Jenny immediately spotted the one she wanted, and she and Loggam went running over to it.

"This is it, Daddy! This is the one I want!" she wailed.

The tree was enormous; it would have been a better pick for Rockefeller Center than the inside of a camper! Ken, Cindy, and Judith all laughed because they've all been through this before.

"Perhaps we will keep looking around, sweetheart. We did just start looking."

Ken, realizing he'd better take the lead on the next suggestion, found a perfectly sized tree that looked healthy and full. "Well, take a look at this one. I think it would fit perfectly. Do you like it, Jenny?"

Jenny walked all around the tree judging its shape, size, and sniff testing until finally she stepped back and gave a nod with a thumbs up. Ken started pulling out his saw and began cutting down the tree. Once he got it secured to his wagon, the search continued until Loggam found the right tree for them. He was very particular on his hunt. He had something exact in his mind that he was looking for, and everyone just followed as he inspected each one.

Finally, after about a half an hour, he spotted his tree. It was a smaller tree that really had seen better days, but this was the one he wanted, he was sure about it. It had bald spots throughout and the lengths of the branches were oddly proportioned. Judith walked over and was equally happy with his choice.

"My son always picks a tree with slight imperfections; he's done this every year. He says it's what makes them perfect."

Both Ken and Cindy liked that, they saw the charm in it. Loggam didn't wait a moment before he pulled out the saw, which was too big for his hands, but he started sawing away. Ken offered to help, but Loggam said it was okay, that he was a pro at it. All by himself, he loaded the tree onto his wagon and roped it securely in so it would make the trip home safely. Ken was so impressed by the will and determination of this young boy. During their walk back to camp, they all decided that they'd decorate one at a time, starting with Jenny's tree.

Ken propped up the tree and put it on the stand in the corner of their camper right by the window. Jenny dumped water into the tree stand so it wouldn't go thirsty, as she put it. Mindy made some popcorn, and they all started stringing strands of it for the tree. Of course, she needed to make more than one bag because both Jenny and Loggam ate most of it! While they did that, Ken hung the lights all around the tree, and when he finished, the popcorn went up next. They brought a box filled with ornaments and tinsel that was added last.

When it was all done, Ken hoisted Jenny onto his shoulders and she added the angel to the top of the tree. While she was up there, Loggam noticed she was whispering something to the angel. He didn't ask her about it when she came down, but he was very curious about what she might have said.

They turned down the lights and took in the beauty of their finished tree. Loggam felt this was the right time to start belting out "Rudolf the Red-nosed Reindeer," and they all joined in!

When it started to get late, Judith and Loggam headed home. Tomorrow, they would be joining them to decorate their tree. Judith felt so blessed to have these new and old friendships because never would there be a lonely Christmas.

The next day, Judith spent the morning making tomato sauce for her big spaghetti and meatball dish later that night. The house smelled delicious as the sauce cooked. She also gathered all their Christmas decorations from the storage cubby. Loggam was up in his room gathering all his rocks so that he could show Jenny his cool collection.

"Loggam, sweetheart, would you gather some wood for later, please? Also when you finish, it's just about time for lunch."

"Okay, Mom. I sure will."

After Loggam brought in some logs, they sat down and had some chicken noodle soup. Judith could tell Loggam had something on his mind; he looked as if he was trying to process his thoughts.

"Hey, Mama," Loggam said thoughtfully. "Why does Jenny look like she does?"

Judith had known Loggam would eventually ask her these questions and be curious about her. She hadn't known much about the diagnosis herself; only that Jenny had a very bad illness.

"Well, sweetheart, do you remember when Steven Johnson, the boy in your class, stopped coming to school for a long time?" Loggam nodded. "Well, Steven had something called leukemia. Leukemia is a form of cancer that affects the blood cells in your body. It makes some of your healthy cells sick, and sometimes it spreads to otherwise healthy areas of your body. Do you remember Mrs. Helene teach you about that?"

"Yes, I do… I remember her saying sometimes they can make it all better, but sometimes they can't. Can they make Jenny's all better?"

Loggam had the most serious expression a nine-year-old possibly could, with his big soft eyes and worried look on his face. Judith wished she could tell her son something to ease his worried heart but she didn't know enough about Jenny's situation to do so. So she told him that together they would pray for Jenny and that miracles happened every day. With that, Loggam got up off his seat and went into a kneel. He folded his hands together and started his conversation with God about his new friend Jenny. Judith joined him on the floor, and together, they prayed for Jenny.

As the evening started to take hold, their new friends, the Mallets, showed up at Judith's front door. They had with them a box of hot chocolate, some whipped cream, and a few ornaments they picked out. Loggam had already set up his unique little tree in front of the big bay window in the living room. They decided they'd sit for dinner first and decorate the tree afterward. As they sat around the table, everyone enjoyed Judith's cooking immensely. Loggam and Jenny were finished first and asked if they could be excused. Loggam was anxious to show Jenny his cool rock collection he's amassed over the years. The two kids cleared their plates and ran up to Loggam's bedroom.

"These are the coolest rocks I've found throughout the woods," Loggam said. Jenny was excited to dig through them. The each kneeled on the floor as he dumped a huge pile across the carpet. Jenny was smiling big as she picked up and looked at each one.

"I love how they sparkle. Ohh, look at this one; it has specks of glitter in it," she said.

"Do you wanna see my favorite?"

"Sure!"

Loggam pulled out his display case and removed his "special" rock. Jenny took it very carefully as if it was fragile. She came across the words written on the front, and she was floored.

"Wow, Loggam. This is special. It's so smooth."

The two of them sat together discussing were he found each one for about fifteen minutes. Loggam excused himself to go use the bathroom, and Jenny was left content to continue her inspection. As Loggam reached the staircase, he overheard Ken speaking to Judith about Jenny. He knew he shouldn't listen; his parents always told him not to eavesdrop on other people's conversations, but he was really worried about his friend. Loggam decided he would just listen for a little while; he carefully sat in a crouched position beside the landing. He couldn't quite make out or fully understand what they were saying. He heard them talk about seeing many different specialists or something called an oncologist. He didn't know what that meant. He also heard them saying the prognosis hadn't been good so far.

Ken was saying the main reason they got away for the holidays was because it had been so sad and disheartening news.

Then Loggam heard what he really knew he shouldn't. It sounded as if Ken was sniffling as the words "They don't think she'll see another Christmas" were somberly spoken. Loggam couldn't even begin to make sense of what he heard. He knew he missed much of the conversation, and even the parts he did get, he didn't understand. His little mind was spinning, trying to put it all together, especially those last words he heard.

He quickly went back to the room and decided his bladder would have to wait. He didn't want to let on to Jenny what he just heard so he went back to talking about his rocks. He watched her more closely now, and it occurred to him the most special thing sitting among his favorite collectibles was her.

A few minutes later, their parents called them down to start decorating the tree. Loggam could tell both Mindy and Judith had just been crying. He knew because whenever his mom would cry about his dad her cheeks would get puffy and her nose would get red. Judith knew her son was very good at reading people and decided she'd pull out the old record player she had and put in Johnny Cash's Christmas album, *They'll Be Peace in the Valley*. They all started humming and singing along, which helped lift the spirits in the room.

After the cocoa was made, they filled their decorative mugs and continued decorating the tree. Most of the ornaments were handmade either by Judith or Loggam. Each one carried so much sentimental value. She had the one from when she and Gus first got married, and then when they first had Loggam. So many memories hung from those limbs. Loggam pulled out his dad's old train set that was wrapped around the floor of the tree every year. His dad saved up each year to buy a new piece to his assembly. It was an old set that his dad had started back when Gus was a young man. Ken was so amazed by it and how perfect the condition of it was. When it was time for the tree topper, Loggam went into his mom's room and came out carrying his dad's old hat. He climbed up his little step stool and placed the hat right on the top of the tree. Judith smiled because Loggam started this new tradition after Gus had passed; he said it was so his dad was also helping them decorate the tree. When it was all finished, it wasn't the prettiest tree ever, but every piece of it was so special to the Maggel family.

After their company went home, Judith and Loggam took a few moments to take in their tree. They said a little prayer once again for Jenny and one for Gus. Judith was unaware that Loggam had heard any part of her conversation the Mallets. "Did you have a good time tonight, Loggam?"

"Yes, Mama. I really did! I really like Jenny a lot, Mama. You know what?"

"What's that dear?"

"I think Jenny is really special. Remember how I told you I felt Daddy was around me when I had my special rock?"

"Yes, I do."

"Well, I feel like that when she is around me too."

"I couldn't agree more. She is very special, sweetheart." Judith hugged her sweet boy so tight and kissed him on his forehead. "Why don't you go wash up for bed, my love."

"Okay, Mama. Good night."

"Good night, hunny."

While Loggam brushed his teeth, he started thinking about his friend Steven in school and how closely he reminded him of what Jenny is going through. The more he kept thinking about it, something like a light bulb flashed in his mind. He recalled Steven would go to see a camper friend of theirs, Dr. Chen. Dr. Chen didn't live far, and even though he was right down the street, he would take his small camper into to state park just for some weekends. Loggam's little brain starting churning he thought maybe if Dr. Chen was able to help Steven, maybe he'd be able to help Jenny.

After he finished getting ready for bed, he slowly went halfway down the stairs and listened for his mom. He didn't hear any sounds at all. He walked into his room and grabbed a piece of paper from his desk and wrote, "Mom, if you see this, I am okay. I had to run out and take care of something really important." He left his note on his bed and slowly and carefully retreated down the steps and out his front door. He stood at the door listening for a moment and then turned on his flashlights and started toward the doctor's house. Loggam knew this weekend the doctor wasn't at the campsite because his usual site by the lake was empty.

As Loggam made his way down the street, it had started to flurry. He loved when it would snow; he prayed for a white Christmas. Loggam lifted his mouth to the air and put out his tongue as he tried to catch snowflakes in his mouth. He did this all the way until he reached the doctor's street.

When he walked up to the house, he noticed lights were on in the house. It was just about nine thirty when he arrived. He tried to think about what he was going to say when he got up to the door. He knocked softly and just waited. Dr. Chen opened the door and was surprised to see little Loggam standing there.

"Loggam, are you okay? Is your mom all right?"

"Yes, sir. We are both fine, but I do need to speak to you about someone else. Mind if I come in?"

Dr. Chen was a surprised by this visit and invited Loggam in. Together, they walked over to the study and had a seat.

"You fixed Steven all up when he was sick, and I have a friend who is very special and needs your help too."

Dr. Chen was a bit bewildered by all this and starting asking Loggam questions. The conversation went on for about ten minutes before he was all filled in on everything at least Loggam knew. "I promise you, son, that tomorrow morning, first thing, I will go meet Jenny personally. Now, does your mother know you've come here?"

"No, sir, but I did leave a note for her if she noticed I was gone."

"Okay, well, I am going to drive you home because I don't want you walking this late yourself as I am sure your mom wouldn't want either."

Dr. Chen drove Loggam back to his house. Upon Loggam's request, he didn't pull all the way into the driveway so he shut his lights off and waited until he watched Loggam walk up and go into the front door. Loggam sneaked in carefully and didn't hear a sound. He slowly made his way back up to his room and crumbled up the note that he'd left just in case. His work was done, and now he felt he could go to sleep.

The following morning went as usual, with breakfast and some small house chores. Loggam loved having a break from school so he could spend his time outdoors as much as possible. That afternoon, they heard a knock at their door. It was Ken, and he was in such good spirits, more so than Loggam had ever seen him have.

"I wanted to come tell you that we won't be able to meet this afternoon for lunch, but it's for a wonderful reason. This morning an oncologist that lives in this area called us. He said he was contacted by a colleague in our hospital in Tennessee and wanted permission to view Jenny's medical background. After I signed and emailed the authorization forms for him to receive her medical records, he called our doctor in Tennessee to ask more questions about her, and they told us we were here! What are the chances of that? It almost seemed too good to be true! After he reviewed her medical records, he said he felt strongly that she would be the perfect candidate for a treatment plan that's had a high success rate! Upon discovering we were actually close to him and not in Tennessee, he requested we come in today. Mindy and Jenny are already at his office now running some tests."

Judith was positively glowing with this news! She wished she'd thought to inquire about Dr. Chen herself; she was amazed at the timing of this too.

"Oh, Ken, that is so amazing! Please keep me informed of how she's doing. I can tell you, Dr. Chen is an amazing doctor. We have friends who have used him before. I wish I'd have thought to tell you about him myself!"

After a few minutes of chit-chat Ken left to go to the doctor's office, and Judith was so pleased to hear the news she had to tell Loggam. After Judith told Loggam the good news, she realized though he acted surprised, something was off about him. She always knew when Loggam had something up his sleeve, but as long as he was okay, she figured in time, she would find out what it was.

Some weeks had passed, and it was finally Christmas Eve. The Mallets had stayed the whole month while Jenny received treatment from Dr. Chen. For the first few weeks, it was difficult to visit her because she was very sick and needed mostly sleep. The last week went totally differently for Jenny. She had a lot more energy and much more color to her face. The dark circles under her eyes seemed to disappear, and she even looked like she had a little more weight on her.

Since Jenny was feeling a lot better, the doctor felt she could return to her family rather than staying at the treatment center any longer, especially being it was Christmas Eve. All Jenny wanted to do was get to see Loggam, so Ken, Mindy, and Jenny gathered themselves together and set off to Judith's cottage. When Judith opened the door to see Jenny standing there looking in so much better shape than she'd ever seen her, she just grabbed her into a hug and bit back tears. She just looked so much healthier, and even though they were waiting for the recent blood test results to reveal the true prognosis, they'd enjoy every moment of Jenny's seemingly good health. They all sat in the living room together as the kids were in their own slice of heaven just being back together. Jenny and Loggam had formed such a special bond over this time together. They all decided they were going to go into town later that night for the annual tree lighting ceremony and then attend midnight mass together. Judith and Mindy put together a quick dinner for their group, and after their bellies were full, they all dressed warm and jumped in Judith's station wagon heading toward town.

When they arrived, the town was lit with color from all the twinkle lights. Each shop had Christmas decorations and beautiful wreaths covering their storefront. There were giant, air-filled reindeer, and a beautiful live nativity scene. The town looked so beautiful. It was a great turn out with vendors serving hot chocolate and caramel apples as well as hot apple cider. There was a choir singing "O Holy Night," and carolers spreading cheer at the other end.

As the bunch walked through, Jenny and Loggam didn't know what to sink their teeth into first. They had a caramel apple then old-fashioned powdered donuts and then apple cider! They spent hours walking around, talking to everyone, and walking in and out of the shops along the street. At 9 PM, they were going to light the Christmas tree. The mayor of the town started speaking shortly before nine and welcomed both the old and the new members, he spoke about the beauty in togetherness and the holidays.

"It has been an honor and privilege to be the mayor of this fine town, and furthermore, to get the joy of lighting our beautiful Christmas tree. This year, I would like to change that up a bit, if you all don't mind. After speaking with a dear friend of mine, he was telling me about a very special young lady he'd met that was new to our town. If she wouldn't mind, I'd like her to come up here and light the tree for us all."

Ken and Mindy had no idea whom they were talking about. They looked down at their little girl's face and had big tears take over their eyes when they saw her expression light up. She was so excited to get to light the big tree! With an "Is it okay?" look to Ken, Loggam grabbed Jenny's hand and started walking her through the crowds toward the stage that held the major. Ken was more than pleased to have Loggam take her up there. Ken and Mindy just gathered together and watched their once energy-less, sickly, baby girl skip with excitement as she made her way up. Whatever was meant to happen in the coming time mattered not in this moment, for this moment they'd treasure forever. Loggam led Jenny up the steps, but he stayed down with the rest of the crowd. Jenny very shyly walked up to the mayor and the whole town clapped for her.

Then the countdown started… "Ten… Nine… Eight… Seven… Six… Five… Four… Three… Two… One!"

At that, she plugged the lights in and marveled at the beautiful tree! Everyone had clapped and started singing "O Christmas Tree."

After more fun and games in town, they all went home to change for midnight mass. They got back in the car around eleven forty-five to head over to the church. The church was decorated beautifully and had a full house. Each pew was full of families and friends Judith and Loggam knew. Their friend, Janice, had saved a pew for them all, knowing they were all coming. Across the way, they saw Dr. Chen and his family too. Ken, Mindy, and Jenny went over and visited with him before mass began. The mass was simply beautiful. Each year, it seemed to get better and better.

Loggam and Jenny started to fall asleep toward the end, and they were both anxious to get home and get to sleep so Santa could come visit them. When Loggam got home, he put out some Oreos and milk for Santa and then some trail mix on the front walk for the reindeer. He had wanted to get up on the roof to make it easier for them, but Judith requested he not do that and said they will fly down to eat it. He jumped into bed and said his prayers. He couldn't wait for morning so he closed his eyes tight and hoped the excitement didn't keep him awake much longer. After about ten minutes, he was sound asleep.

Christmas morning, Loggam jumped out of bed with the morning light. He ran down his steps into his mom's room and jumped in her bed!

"It's Christmas, Mommy! It's Christmas!" He grabbed her covers and peeled her out of them.

Sleepily, Judith got up, put on her robe and went out to the tree with Loggam. Loggam reached first for the gift he got for his mom rather than one of his own. He gave it to her with such pride and enthusiasm. She held the carefully wrapped gift with a bow made from paper and read the label.

"Mama, love you to the moon and back, Loggam."

She opened her gift to reveal a small red velvet box. Inside the box was a locket shaped into a heart. She opened the heart to reveal a picture of Gus on one side and a picture of Loggam in the other. She had no clue how he could pay for that or who made it for him. She was so touched by this beautiful gift.

"Oh sweetheart, it is beautiful... I will wear it always."

Loggam started tearing into his presents. He received new pajamas that Judith had sewn for him, another rock display case, and a set of Legos, a movie he's wanted, and a few other little knickknacks. His big gift from Santa was a new bike! He was so happy that he started riding it through the house!

He had one last gift under the tree. He reached under and read the label.

"To my sweet boy, from Daddy."

Loggam's eyes welled up with tears and he just kept reading it over and over again. He knew his father's handwriting and knew that it was his.

"Is this really from Daddy, Mama?"

"Yes, sweetheart. He wrapped this and told me to give it to you when you had gotten a little bit older."

Loggam carefully unwrapped the gift, keeping the label unaffected so he could keep it. Inside was a gold pocket watch which an inscription on it. It read, "To my special boy."

"You see, Loggam, your father received that watch from his father. That inscription he added for you."

"Mama, I love it! It's like the rock I carved special into that made me think of daddy!"

"Yes, sweetheart. I took that as a sign from your dad he wanted me to give you his watch."

"I will take good care of it, Mama."

"I know you will, sweetheart, as I will my new locket."

The only gifts that remained under the tree were the ones for Mindy, Ken, and Jenny. They were coming over later that day to have a Christmas feast together.

That afternoon Ken, Mindy, and Jenny showed up at Judith's door with a car full of items to bring in. First, a beautiful wreath with glittery silver pine cones was hung on the front door. They also had presents and a big crate filled with food. They decided they'd cook first and the kids set the table while talking about what Santa brought for them. Loggam said the reindeer ate all the trail mix he left out for them, and Santa only left half of one cookie. Jenny said Santa ate all her oatmeal cookies and left a tiny bit of milk. Jenny left carrots out for the reindeer and was pleased to see they were all gone when she had checked for them. The kids were in their bliss talking and comparing Santa's visit.

The table was set and filled with yummy food. They had roast beef, mashed potatoes, string beans, cranberry and some biscuits. They all said a prayer of thanks before digging into the food.

Just as everyone's plates were just about empty, there was a knock at the front door. Loggam went over and opened it to find Dr. Chen standing there.

"Merry Christmas, everyone! I am sorry to just stop in like this, but I was hoping to speak with Ken and Mindy before I left this evening to go out of town."

"Merry Christmas, Doctor. Please come on in," Judith said.

Ken and Mindy walked over to the kitchen with Dr. Chen, and the rest of them stayed at the table to give them privacy.

"Again, I am sorry to come at Christmas, but this couldn't wait. I have to tell you, even as a doctor, I am a bit surprised by what has happened."

Both Ken and Mindy were fearful and eager to hear what fate had in store for Jenny. "Please tell us, Doctor," Ken said.

"I think we've had a bit of a Christmas miracle because your daughter has a clean bill of health. Every recent test, I have gone over with a fine-tooth comb, and cancer does not exist anywhere in her body."

Both Ken and Mindy didn't speak—they couldn't. they cried out and held one another so tight even Dr. Chen had tears in his eyes.

"We will continue monitoring her progress, even when you get home. I've already counseled with her doctor and we've discussed it thoroughly."

Ken just grabbed Dr. Chen into a huge bear hug and sobbed into his shoulder, "Thank you, Doctor. Oh God, thank you… you've given us our baby girl back."

Dr. Chen hugged him back just as tight and said, "I can't take all the credit for that. There is something you two should know." Ken and Mindy stood back and listened. "The night before I showed up at your door, I wasn't going through case studies."

Both Ken and Mindy were bewildered by this and grew more intrigued. "Well, I was visited by someone who made it very clear to me I needed to meet your Jenny. He was rather insistent. The catalyst that started the ball rolling was Loggam. He explained what a special girl she was and that she needed my help right away. I just felt you should know that.

"Now here is all the paperwork, you have my number and can call me anytime. I will be visiting with her in a few weeks to see how she's doing but you have a 100 percent cancer-free, healthy young girl."

With that, Mindy and Ken hugged and thanked him repeatedly and he left. Both Ken and Mindy looked into the dining room at their baby. They just stood there and stared at her.

"Our baby is going to be okay. She's going to grow up and live out her dreams," Mindy said. They embraced one final time before making their way back to the table.

Jenny, Loggam, and Judith were all so curious as to what happened. They heard some commotion but really weren't sure if that was good or not. Jenny walked over to her parents, and they knelt to her level.

"Jenny, my love, you aren't sick anymore, sweetheart. The doctor was just here with all your results, and they all came back perfect," Mindy said with tears running down her cheeks.

"I'm going to be okay then?" Jenny asked.

"Yes. A hundred percent. We will still go to the doctors for checkups, but Dr. Chen has made it very clear that you are healthy!"

Ken scooped Jenny up in his arms and kissed her face in a million places! Mindy grabbed onto them both and did the same. Judith and Loggam watched with tears in both their eyes. Loggam was saying prayers of thanks for this was his true Christmas wish.

Loggam decided he didn't want to wait any longer to give his gift to Jenny. He walked over to the tree and pulled it out from underneath. Judith, Ken, and Mindy stood in the background and watched. Loggam took Jenny's hand, and they both sat by the tree on the living-room floor. Jenny had her gift for Loggam ready to go as well and she asked if she could go first. Loggam ripped away the paper to find a rock polishing kit! He had never seen one before and he loved it! Inside was also a little black velvet bag. He reached in the bag and pulled out a giant green crystal. This was like no rock he had and it shined and glittered across every service. Loggam flipped it over to the flattened side and engraved into it was the words *best friend*. He loved it so much he grabbed Jenny in for a huge hug! She'd received many of those so far today!

Loggam handed her his present for her next. She unwrapped the paper to reveal a long rectangular box. Inside was a beautiful antique purple hairbrush with a little note that read, "You will use this again soon. Love, Loggam." Jenny stared at the brush, and it occurred to her she would have her hair again!

She looked up at her mom and dad and said, "Will I really have my hair back?"

Mindy knelt next to her daughter, kissed the tear shedding onto her small cheek and said, "Yes, you will."

As Jenny marveled at the brush she realized something else was in the corner of the box. She reached in and removed her last gift from Loggam, it was the "special" rock that he coveted more than any other he had. She instantly felt just as the rock said, special. Jenny wrapped Loggam in a huge hug and even kissed his freckled cheek. Loggam blushed a little but was very pleased that she was happy with his gift.

As the children finished up, Judith gave her gift to Jenny next. It was a beautiful handmade scarf and matching sweater. Judith also made one for Mindy. She made Ken a pair of warm gloves. Mindy and Ken got Judith a beautiful clock for her mantel. They also got Loggam a new red wagon to replace the one he had, which had a loose wheel. As they all sat in the living room thanking one another for the beautiful and thoughtful gifts, Ken wanted to say a few words.

"This has truly been the most special Christmas we've ever had and will go down as the best. We've received so many blessings." With tears in his eyes, he continued. "Not only have we received the news that our baby is healthy but also have welcomed new members to our family."

Ken walked over to Loggam and knelt in front of him, with tears streaming down his face. "Loggam, Dr. Chen told us what you did. We know that you are the one who went to see him about Jenny, and you will never know how eternally grateful we are. Your father would be so proud of the young man you've become."

Judith was stunned hearing this, as she did not know about this either. She was always proud of the kind-hearted boy she had, but this was certainly one of those proud mom moments for her. Ken shook Loggam's hand and pulled him into a hug.

"You are a part of this family, Loggam. Thank you for being my daughter's guardian angel," Mindy said.

Loggam was very touched by Ken and Mindy's words but, most of all, just happy that his best friend Jenny was going to be okay. In his mind, his Christmas wish and prayers were answered. Loggam would be seeing a lot more of Jenny for years and years to come; he knew in his heart this was just the beginning of their story.

Part Two

Loggam Maggel Meets
the Deegan Family

It was a crisp, cool morning in Red Fir Mountain State Park. Loggam was sure to dress warm and grab his heavier coat and gloves that day. As he pulled his front door open, he took a big breath in.

"Ahh, smells like it's going to snow today."

Loggam always loved the change of seasons and the new weather they'd bring. He started on his path to collect some logs and visit his friends. Once he had a good stack, he decided he'd hit his first site where the Loveries stayed. Loggam walked up, and to his disappointment, the class C camper was gone and a new camper was there. He always was happy to welcome newcomers to the campsite so he decided he'd knock on the door and introduce himself. He figured they can use the firewood anyhow.

A tall man with dark-brown curly hair opened the door.

"Good morning, sir. My name is Loggam Maggel, and I wanted to come introduce myself. I live here on the grounds. I thought maybe you could use some firewood."

"Well, thank you, Loggam. We certainly appreciate that. Speaking of firewood, what would you recommend is the best spot for a campfire?"

"Well, there are certainly many to choose from, but over by Skully Lake there is a beautiful spot with a firepit all ready to go. I keep the firewood stacked tall over there, so you don't need to bring any of this with you."

"Would you care to join us later? We're going to have a cookout with hot dogs and hamburgers"

"That sounds great."

"By the way, my name is Peter, my wife's Hannah, and our daughter's Cassy, and our youngest is Pete Jr."

"Well, Peter, it was very nice to meet you, and I look forward to seeing you all later."

Loggam left Peter's site and started making his rounds visiting friends along his path. As he went along, he cleared the brush out of the bike path and reached into his pockets, pulled out ample handfuls of coins, to which he scattered along the ground.

Some hours later, Loggam started on the return trip toward home. He knew his mom would be looking out for him for lunch. Loggam and his mother lived very simplistic lives. They had lived quite modestly for most of Loggam's life, but that had all changed suddenly after a gift left by a fellow camper. It was a lottery ticket, and not just any lottery ticket, but one that would turn Loggam into a millionaire! Wealth meant very little to Loggam, as he had everything he could ever really need or want out of life. One thing he had decided to do with his money, however, was to build his mother a beautiful log cabin right outside of Red Fir Mountain State Park. It wasn't an enormous cabin by any stretch of the word, and though he hired on a few friends, he chose to build it himself. He put extra care and attention in his mother's room and the kitchen; as all women know, the kitchen is the heart of the home. One of his mother's favorite things to do was bake. Growing up, she didn't have the luxury to do it much because money was tight and resources were few and far between. When she'd first been married to Loggam's father, Gus, she'd spent hours in the kitchen baking up a storm. It was her true happy place. Sadly, Gus had passed away when Loggam was only seven years old. Judith made it her single devotion to provide Loggam a happy, enriched life. She took him camping and fishing regularly, they built forts in the leaves and played hide and go seek and kick the can. And when he was at school, she worked for the campground, answering phones and booking reservations to make ends meet. They never did have much money, but that never stopped them from using their creativity to create a world full of imagination and laughter.

As anticipated when Loggam walked in the door, the smell of apple pie hit him instantly. Judith was in her bliss pulling pie and cookies out of the oven. Something about the cool weather always had her baking continuously.

"Hello, Mom. Something sure smells good in here!"

"Hello, Loggam. How was your morning?"

"Great. I met some new friends over at the Loveries' site. They invited me to a cookout later tonight, would you like to join me?"

"Tonight, I am meeting with the book club, but do bring this pie with you when you go."

"Thanks, Mom. I sure will do that."

After grabbing a few hot cookies, Loggam grabbed the turkey sandwich his mom had made for him and sat and had lunch with her. The two of them enjoyed one another's company and got caught up in conversation about gathering supplies for the local food drive. Loggam always chose to stay actively involved within his community, and now that he had the means to do it, he donated regularly to many causes.

Later that day, he gathered a bag filled with hot chocolate packets, two bags of huge marshmallows, and his mom's freshly made apple pie and headed out to the Deegans' campsite. When he arrived at the family's camper, he knocked on the door and had them follow him along to the firepit and BBQ grill beside Skully Lake.

Immediately, the fellow campers could see why Loggam chose this spot. It was stunning, to say the least. With the sun setting in the sky, it was like a kaleidoscope exploding with colors of pink, blue, orange, and purple. The trees were lively as the danced in the breeze and it seemed they went on forever. No matter which direction you looked, the view was simply breathtaking. When Peter finally moved from his spot of awe, he went over to the grill and fired it up.

In the midst of grilling the chow, Peter Jr. suddenly exclaimed, "*Look, Daddy. Look!*" Pete Jr. sifted through the leaves and pulled out a shiny silver dollar. He was so enthralled by his discovery.

Cassy came over and immediately was taken aback, "*Look, I see more!*" She pulled out three quarters and two dimes.

"Well, how do you suppose those got there?" Pete Sr. said.

"I'm going to keep looking!" exclaimed both Cassy and Pete Jr. Loggam did his best to contain the big grin across his cheeks; nothing brought him more pleasure then to watch the excitement across the children's faces as they made their discoveries and went on a hunt for more treasure.

As the children used the rest of the sunlight to search for their treasure, Loggam, Pete, and Hannah continued setting up the food and got to know each other better. "So, where are you all from?" Loggam asked.

"Oh, we are here from Charleston, South Carolina. I work for the electric company and save up all my vacation so we can hit a new destination every year with our camper."

"Wow, South Carolina. I've seen pictures of South Carolina; it's a beautiful place."

"Yes, it is, but every now and then we like to get out and explore different areas."

"What brought you here to Alabama?" Loggam noticed Hannah had a gloomy expression on her face.

"Well," Pete said. "Friends of ours had told us about this place and said that their children had a heck of a time. In fact, they don't want to go anywhere else but here."

"Is that so? Well, I guess our little town has a way of growing on people. I know I have lived here all my life, never been outside the state line and don't have much desire to."

Cassy and Pete Jr came rushing back to show their parents all the treasure they unearthed. "Look at all we found, Dad! It's so heavy!"

"Well, I'll be, kids. I told you that this place had a little magic. That's what the Browns told us, right?"

"We're gonna keep looking while we have a little light left!"

With that, they were off, and Pete was shocked because the kids did manage to find a generous amount of coins on the ground.

"Hey, Loggam, you don't think someone accidently dropped all that, do ya?"

"I can safely say anyone who dropped that did it quite intentionally."

Both Pete and Hannah looked at one another hesitantly before Hannah took a deep breath and started speaking. "If I can be candid with you, our children haven't had the easiest of times. We came here because a few weeks ago, we lost our home to a fire. We are still waiting to hear back if it's at all salvageable or not. Not only were both of my children brought to that house as infants, I was as well. My father helped build that house. Every corner held such fond memories. Our little Peter lost his favorite teddy bear, Moe. I think he was more devastated over that. We wanted to get the kids away from all the sadness so good friends of ours insisted we come here."

"We haven't seen them smile this much in what feels like a very long time," Pete said.

Loggam's heart hung heavy upon hearing what struggles this family was enduring. "I am so very sorry to hear all you've been through, and I am glad you are here for now and that the children have this time. If you'd prefer, we don't need to have a campfire, I can see how that might not be enjoyable for your family at this time."

"It's important we do," Hannah said. "See, and we don't want the children, or even us for that matter, afraid of fire for the rest of their lives. We want them to be able to enjoy themselves."

"Well," Loggam said. "I think that is a good idea, and we will show these kids a wonderful time."

After some more conversation, the food was all ready and they all sat across the picnic tables, eating their hot dogs and hamburgers. Loggam pulled out the apple pie and everyone's mouths watered, wanting to cut into it.

As the darkness took over the sky, Loggam showed the kids how he could rub two sticks together and make fire. They were awestruck and thought he was the coolest man they'd ever seen after that. They watched as the fire blazed and danced in the breeze. They sat around it with Cassy and Pete Jr. sitting right beside Loggam. They listened to his stories fervently as he told them campfire tales. Then he pulled out the marshmallows, and once again, won big points with the children. When it started getting late Loggam helped the Deegan family pack up their belongings and head back to their site. After ensuring they made it back okay, he headed back home spilling coins from his pockets along the way.

As Loggam walked through his front door, his mind was churning once again. He couldn't believe what that sweet family had to endure. He got to work quickly mapping out a plan. First, he needed the phone book and then he put pen to paper. Hours later, he was satisfied with his strategy and went to bed.

The next morning, Loggam woke up with exuberance. He had much to get done today and no time to wait. He started with his phone calls and didn't stop until lunch. When he hung up the phone, he had a warm grin on his cheeks. Loggam kept all his planning to himself.

He went down to the kitchen and joined his mom for lunch. Today they had tomato soup with grilled cheese; it was one of his favorites.

"You were quite busy this morning?" Judith said.

"Oh, I had some work to do, a few calls to make."

Judith never was one to pry; she knew whatever her son had up his sleeve was personal.

"Would you like to join me today and meet the Deegan family? They are gonna be here until the end of the week."

"I'd love to. Let me just get my shortbread cookies ready to go."

Loggam and his mom set off to the site that held the Deegan family. Once they arrived, Pete was on his cell phone just ending a conversation with someone. "Well, hello there, Loggam. Good of you to come back, and who do we have here?"

"Pete, this is my mother, Judith."

"It's good to meet you, Judith, we've had such a wonderful time getting to know your boy here. I think our kids want to take him home with us! We would love it if you joined us on our hike today, and we figured we'd find a nice spot for dinner later too."

"We would enjoy that."

The Deegans and the Maggels had spent hours walking through the beautiful trails and admiring the majestic mountains. They'd seen beautiful wildlife along their trek, and of course, the children collected coins along the way. As sunset struck they decided to BBQ beside Locklier Mountain; it was a magnificent spot. Loggam once again entertained the children and parents with stories about these woods and fellow campers who'd visited previously.

During their walk, back to the site, Pete was telling Loggam about his phone call earlier. "Well, they told us we should come back in three weeks rather than this Saturday to see what we can possibly salvage from the remains. We've just been having such a wonderful time here, I fear what we will return to. Then we must start house hunting. I don't think my wife will ever find anything that will feel like home again. It will be nice to get the extra time here."

"You keep your chin up, Pete. You have a beautiful family, and I know in my heart you will all get through this."

The following days and nights were spent with the Deegans. In such a short amount of time, they felt like family. They spent the whole trip talking, laughing, and playing with the kids. Loggam introduced them to "kick the can," that really kept them entertained, even for Loggam too! Judith kept their bellies full of homemade sweets; she loved having people to bake for.

As Saturday approached, they didn't want to leave, and Loggam and Judith were sad to see them go. But once you visit Red Fir Mountain State Park, it becomes a part of you, and you could never truly stay away too long. Loggam knew he'd see them again soon. All the goodbyes were exchanged, and the kids had tears coming down their eyes, they didn't want to leave. The camper pulled down the road, and Loggam smiled and waved.

As the Deegans approached their former street, anxiety and sadness started to take hold. Pete held Hannah's hand to lend emotional support, as he knew this was hardest for her to see. As they turned the final corner and their house came into view, Pete just slammed on his breaks and his jaw dropped! He thought he was hallucinating because before his very eyes was their house in perfect condition—even better than it had been before the fire. Every last detail was exactly as they'd left it even down to the striping on the shudders.

He pulled the RV into the driveway, and they all filed out awestruck. Everyone was silent as their eyes traveled every inch of the home. The details of the home were the same yet a few added pieces had been thrown in. A basketball net was added to the driveway, the landscaping was flawlessly beautiful with colorful flowers and a Japanese maple tree in the front yard. After about twenty minutes of just standing there taking it all in, they decided to walk into the home.

"This can't be!" exclaimed Hannah as she cried her eyes out. Everything was exactly the same with once again some added touches. Sitting on the bench across from the front door was a square block of concrete that came from the front sidewalk. It had Hannah's handprint from when she was only six years old. She held that to her chest and smiled remembering when her father and her did that. She couldn't believe that survived the fire, or how any of it did.

They walked through the kitchen and found their cabinets stocked with food, their fridge full, and brand-new appliances. They once again didn't know which direction to turn because they were planted in shock and amazement.

Pete Jr. ran to his room and started exclaiming in happiness. Pete, Hannah, and Cassy all went running to see what it was. They stood in the doorway, once again, amazed. Pete Jr's room was the coolest thing they'd ever seen. It was converted into looking like a forest with a mural on the wall and decorations all around, even his ceiling was lit with glow-in-the-dark stars. Sitting on his bed was the really prize though…it was Moe! Pete Jr. ran to his bed and grabbed that bear and hugged it with all he had. Hannah and Pete just looked at one another and cried. They didn't understand at all how this all happened.

Cassy grabbed their hands and now was anxious to get to her room. When she arrived, she was positively giddy! Her room had become a princess' castle. Her bed had a beautiful shimmering pink canopy and was shaped like Cinderella's coach. Those walls were colored in a mint pink with a beautiful chandelier hanging in the center.

Her closet was full of new clothes and princess costumes. She had a wall of books and stories, which was her favorite thing to do! Pete and Hannah walked into their room and once again awestruck with what they saw. They know had a walk-in closet and an en suite with a huge garden tub. The decor was exactly as they liked it and the furnishings were stunning. When they finally made their way down to the kitchen they just sat at the beautiful new center island in sheer wonder.

"I don't... I can't..." Pete was at a complete loss for words. He'd come here with the intent to dig through rubble and see if even one keepsake was in good shape. They expected total ruin. They'd only been gone such a short time; how could this even be done in that time frame.

"Pete, what's that on the stove? It looks like an envelope?"

Pete ran over and grabbed it and tore into it quickly. The contents inside left more questions than answers but also a warm feeling had come over him. Inside were three words, "Pay it forward," and that was it. They decided they weren't going to spend any more time in bewilderment for now and just take it all in. They all came together in the living room and thanked God for this amazing blessing that they had received. The four of them held one another so tight in a sweet embrace and just felt enveloped by warmth.

The next day, the kids went into their backyard and hadn't even noticed when they'd first got home the day before that a huge jungle gym swing set was set up! They ran over to it and started playing on everything they could get their hands on! Pete and Hannah came outside and watched their children's merriment. Suddenly, while in full swing, Pete Jr. jumped off and looked at the leaves on the ground. He moved a few out of the way to reveal coins strewn all through the leaves. Cassy quickly joined him searching the ground for more coins. Pete and Hannah walked over to see what the kids were looking at.

"Look, Mom! We found all these coins on the ground, just like at Red Fir!"

With that, Hannah and Pete looked at one another and everything sank in. The words "Pay it forward" echoed in their heads and in the moment, they decided they were going to do just that.

Together as a family, they started volunteering at their local food kitchen. On weekends, they work within the community to help end hunger by organizing food drives and fundraisers. They never realized what joy they were missing out on in their lives before they started doing this. It brought such a happiness and fulfilment to the Deegan family. What they were even more excited about was they planned a whole month trip to Red Fir Alabama to see their dearest friend and guardian angel, Loggam.

Part Three

Loggam's Summer of Surprises

It was the last half day of school before the summer break officially started. Loggam enjoyed his school days for the most part but was eager for summer to begin. He got along with all his teachers and fellow classmates; it was more the walls around him that made him antsy. He wanted to be with his trees, mountains, and lakes. He felt most at peace when he was outside in his element.

"Now, class, I'd like you to pick up the list by the door with the summer reading list. When you return in the fall, we will be discussing the books in detail. Please do not wait until the last moment to get them started. Have a wonderful and safe summer," Mrs. Brown said both sternly and cheerfully.

The bell rang and total mayhem broke out all over the classroom! People threw papers in the air and ran out the door as if it was a fire alarm that went off. Loggam gathered his things and smirked. Though he was ready to be out the door, he wasn't going to try to get through the cluster of people pushing their way out. So he took the moment to talk to Mrs. Brown.

"Thank you, Mrs. Brown, for a great year. I look forward to reading some of the books on the list. I have already read a few of them."

With a smile on her face, Mrs. Brown replied, "I am sure you have, Loggam. you've always been one of my most eager students."

"Thank you. I hope you have a nice summer, Mrs. Brown!"

"You too, Loggam. I may see you at the summer festival at Red Fir Park too."

"Great! It's going to be the best this year!" Loggam replied. Now that the class had emptied out, Loggam waved and made his way through the door, and summer break officially began!

Loggam climbed down the steps of the bus to his street. It was a tight dirt road right outside of Red Fir State Park so the bus couldn't fit driving down it. That was more than fine with Loggam; he enjoyed walking to his house anyway. He started thinking about all the friends he'd see this summer. Throughout the year, Red Fir Park would welcome many visitors, but the summer held most of them. Loggam walked up the red bricks leading toward his front door. Inside, his mother, Judith, waited for him with food ready to go.

"Hey, Mom. I'm home."

"How was your last day of eighth grade?" Judith said excitingly.

"It was good."

"Glad to hear it. I made some macaroni salad for you. It's waiting on the counter."

Loggam loved his mom's homemade macaroni salad. This was another perk of the summer for him. He could eat that day and night and never grow sick of it! As Loggam piled the food in his mouth, he heard the faint hum of a bus in the distance. He knew it wasn't his school bus as they only stopped over this way for him. He quickly scarfed down the last bit of his food and told his mom he was heading outside. He started walking over toward Red Fir to see what bus came through.

As he arrived, he saw a big blue school bus with *St. Lawrence School for Boys* written across the side. It looked like about fifteen or so kids around his age were standing around the bus collecting their gear. There were enough tents and duffle bags to signify they were staying awhile. One of the boys noticed Loggam and walked over.

"Hello," he said.

"Hello," Loggam returned.

"My name is Trevor. We just got here from Virginia. Most of us are boy scouts back home. We're staying here until right after the summer festival! Do you live around here?"

"Yes, I live right down the street. You guys will love it here. There are some great fishing and cool trails you could take. There is a firepit I built over by Skully Lake too. If you need anyone to show you around while you're here, I'm your man."

"Oh cool, I'd love to see the firepit! We are going to go set up our tents, would you like to come and meet my friends? they'd also like to hear all about the best places to explore. Are you a boy scout too?" Trevor asked.

Loggam had wanted to join the scouts, but the day he was going to ask him mom, he changed his mind. He knew she would do everything she could to send him, but they really didn't have the money to do it. Besides, there wasn't much he could learn as a scout that these woods hadn't taught him already.

"Ah no, I am not, but I'd love to tell you and your friends about this place."

"Okay, cool. Come on."

Trevor walked Loggam over to where a group of boys was standing. The group looked over to Loggam and they all sized one another up before Trevor introduced him to them.

"Hey, guys, this is Loggam. He lives here and knows a lot about the park. He offered to show us some cool places and good fishing spots."

After Trevor spoke, all the boys seemed happy to meet Loggam and introduced themselves. Loggam knew it was unlikely he'd remember all their names and would try his best to match new names with new faces. They all started picking up their gear and asked Loggam to point them in the best direction to make camp. He happily led the way to a spot close to Locklier Mountain that he thought they'd really like.

As planned, when all the boys arrived, they were spinning around to look at everything. Each dropped their tents where they'd be setting them up and just looked around. Loggam noticed that among the group of kids that looked about his age, there were three older guys that he assumed they oversaw the group. He walked over to them and started talking. They all thanked him for finding the location for camp and told him to stick around as much as he liked during their trip. They said they could use his expertise since they were just going off brochure maps they had of the place. They asked Loggam if he'd take them all to the firepit by Skully Lake later that evening. He was happy to do so and figured he'd go home first and tell his mom about the boys he met.

"Bye, guys. I'll see you all later" Loggam said.

"Bye, Loggam!" the group yelled back.

As the evening colors burst across the sky, Loggam left his house to head to the boys' campground. His feet knew this trip well so he was happy to gaze up at the colorful sky along his journey. When Loggam arrived, the boys were eager to head to Skully Lake. They each had gear to bring along, including marshmallows, hotdogs, bug spray, flashlights, and pocket knives.

"Come along this way, guys. I know a shortcut to get us there."

Loggam gathered large pieces of wood and tossed them into the firepit. Before he could show his cool trick to start the fire, two boys already beat him to it. As Loggam recently learned, the boys named Charlie and Dylan were rubbing two sticks together, and after a short amount of time, a small flame appeared. Loggam was impressed seeing the boys do that because more often than not, he was the one bedazzling fellow campers on his fire trick. The group sat around the open flames and told stories about other fires and trips they'd been on. Since all the boys knew one another, Loggam felt slightly left out, not having been on any of the journeys he was listening to. The boy to his right, named Eric, seemed to have noticed and did his best to include Loggam in the conversation and ask him questions.

Loggam quickly liked Eric and felt a kinship with him. The two of them had a lot in common: they both loved the woods and enjoyed the same music and were both the only child in their families. As Loggam and Eric continued getting to know one another, Loggam noticed one of the boys pointing at him and laughing while whispering into Charlie's ear. Charlie didn't seem to engage in the laughter and looked slightly uncomfortable. Loggam hadn't been introduced to this boy nor did he think he wanted to. It seemed like the boys acted kind of strangely around him, slightly timid and wary. Loggam looked at it almost like a wolf pack, and Trent, as they called him, was their alpha. Charlie seemed to be Trent's go-to guy so I suppose he'd be the beta. Loggam enjoyed the company of boys around his age, but he decided he'd steer clear of Trent because he didn't like the vibe he was getting from him.

"You have a really silly name" Trent said. Loggam knew Trent was talking to him as he was looking directly at him.

"I like my name just fine," Loggam replied.

Talking back to Trent seemed to anger him, and with that, he stood to his feet, pointing his finger at Loggam and said, "You don't even go to our school, why are you here? We don't like outsiders much, plus you never were even a boy scout. You probably don't even know how to tie a square knot or even climb a tree! You're just a boy from the woods. You're a woodchuck!" Some of the other boys laughed, as Eric stayed stone-faced. Loggam was both embarrassed and angry; he'd never had a person be so rude to him. His mother always taught him to disregard people like this and kill 'em with kindness, as she'd say. Loggam didn't want to be kind though, he wanted to tie a square knot and climb the highest tree just to prove Trent wrong.

Before Loggam could react or say anything, Ben, one of the counselors, walked up to say it was getting late and time to head back to camp. Trent just gave Loggam a devilish grin knowing Ben didn't overhear him, and he got away with it, not to mention had the last word.

"Hey, Loggam," Eric said. "Listen, I know Trent can be kind of a jerk sometimes. He used to pick on me all the time. He finally stopped when John joined the group, and he started picking on him. I just ignore him."

Loggam thought about what Eric was telling him and was upset by it all. "Eric, you shouldn't have allowed Trent to treat you that way, he doesn't have the right to do that. Thanks for saying this to me, but I will figure out a way to handle it. Maybe tomorrow I will try to talk to him and let him get to know me. Maybe then, he wouldn't be so rude."

"Good luck, Loggam. He can get really nasty sometimes. And just a heads up, he's the prank master so watch your back, Loggam. If he sets his sights for you, all bets are off."

Loggam nodded, shook Eric's hand and headed for home. He'd figure out a way to approach Trent the next day.

The next morning, Loggam woke bright and early. He loved lying in his bed for a few minutes and listening to all the birds chirping right outside his window. The sun's rays splashed across his room through his curtains as he watched the shadows it made dance across his floor. He loved summer mornings. As he finally gathered himself, he threw on a pair of old wrangler jeans, a flannel tea shirt, and his dad's old John Deere hat. He always liked wearing an article of clothing that was his dad's. It made him feel close to him and as if he was still around. He went to the kitchen for some breakfast and found his mom already awaiting him with a bowl of cinnamon apple oatmeal.

"Good morning, Mom."

"Good morning, hun. How'd you sleep?"

"Oh, I slept great, the birds were at my window again this morning. Today, I am going to meet the group and join them on a hike. I met this boy named Eric I really like. We have a lot in common too."

"Well, that's wonderful, you should bring him back here for dinner one night. How long are they here for?"

"Until right after the summer festival."

"Well, make sure you pack some snacks for yourself. I just bought you nutri-grain bars."

"Ohh, did you get strawberry?" Loggam asked with excitement.

"Yes, of course, I did, but I also got the apple cinnamon ones too. I have some exciting news for you too, Loggam."

Loggam loved surprises and sat at the end of his chair waiting to hear.

"I got a phone call yesterday from Ken and Mindy Mallet; they are coming to visit this summer. They will be here next Friday with Jenny."

Loggam jumped up off his seat in excitement! Jenny had quickly become one of Loggam's best friends since they were nine years old. Jenny had been very sick when Loggam first met her, and through his help, she found the doctor who would help become healthy again. Ever since then, Jenny and her family would visit Red Fir as often as they could. Jenny and Loggam were active pen pals and would send an old black and white composition notebook back and forth. They've already filled a few of them over the years. Judith thought it was such a cool idea to stay in touch, and she was so happy Loggam had fostered such a beautiful friendship with Jenny.

"I am so excited to see them, Mom! I wasn't sure if she was coming this summer or not, she hadn't mentioned it last time I got the book. This is going to be the best summer ever!" Loggam scooped up the last mouthful of oatmeal and grabbed his belongings and set out to the woods with a big grin on his face. It his mind, his summer was perfect now that he knew Jenny would be here soon.

As he approached the camp the first person to greet him was Trent. "What are you doing here woodchuck? Didn't I make it clear last night we didn't want you here?"

Loggam took a deep breath and tried not to get frustrated. "I don't know what your problem with me is Trent? I'd like to get to know you, I think we can be friends if you'd give me the chance?"

"Ha! Be your friend? Some poor kid from the woods who couldn't even become a real boy scout?"

With this commotion now being made, Ben walked up just to hear the tail end of Trent's words. "Trent Milford, you do *not* speak to people that way. Where is your code of honor? You will lose privileges this trip as well as merit badges. You will apologize to Loggam right now. As for tonight's scary story night, you will no longer get to participate."

Trent's face turned beet red, and anyone can tell he was very angry. With the least sincerity, he could muster, he apologized to Loggam and walked over to his friends sitting by the tent. Loggam didn't have a good feeling about this. He kind of wished Ben hadn't done that because any chance he had at burying the hatchet with this guy just went away. Eric walked over to Loggam and the two of them started walking in the opposite direction, Loggam told Eric everything that just happened.

All the boys put their packs on and started hiking up the mountainside. They'd stop at different trees and point out interesting parts of the landscape. Loggam, knowing the woods as well as he did, showed the group some fascinating formations along the mountain. He had them follow him off the trail several times to check out different things. With the exception of Trent, all the boys, as well as Ben, were fortunate he was with them as they'd never have seen half of what they did without him. After hiking for a few hours, the boys looked for a place to stop for lunch. They each popped a squat, wiped the sweat from their faces and dug into their lunch. Loggam enjoyed getting to know some of the other guys along the hike. It was so nice for him to be around boys his own age that also appreciated the outdoors as much as he did.

Once lunch was finished Loggam took them over to his favorite climbing tree. He'd especially wanted to do this to show Trent just how well he could "actually climb." Almost like a squirrel, he made his way up the tree, climbing limb from limb with little effort. Eric was so impressed and tried following Loggam but with a little less speed and confidence. Loggam straddled one of the tallest branches and waved back to them at the bottom. He had a big grin on his face as he waved at Trent. Trent folded his arms across his chest and looked completely unimpressed. On his way down, Loggam's hat fell to the ground, and Trent was the first to notice this. He slipped over to the hat while Loggam was distracted coming down the tree. Trent quickly lifted the hat and tucked it away into his bag when no one was looking. He walked over to the group of boys and acted, as he'd been there the whole time. Loggam made his final jump to the ground and started looking for his hat. He asked the other boys if they'd seen it on the ground. They all said no, Eric was looking all over the place as he could tell this hat was important to Loggam.

"I'm sorry, Loggam. I didn't find it anywhere and do you think the wind could have carried it away?"

Loggam was deeply saddened as that was his dad's hat, and he had worn it all the time. It was a very prized possession of Loggam's. Ben asked the group to look all around the trees; each boy lifted rocks and slid their fingers through the leaves and grass, but to no avail. After almost an hour looking, it was a lost cause. Wherever the hat had gone, it was nowhere to be found. The boys started heading back toward camp, as it would take them a good few hours to get back. It was a somber walk back for Loggam, and he didn't say much to the other guys. It took everything he had not to cry, but he certainly wouldn't do that in front of a bunch of guys. He told himself he'd come back and look for the hat himself. Loggam decided he would just head home after they arrived back to camp; he was pretty upset still and didn't really feel like trying to mask it anymore. With the exception of Trent, they all thanked him for showing them around and apologized that he lost his hat. None of the boys but Eric had known that was his father's hat. They said their goodbyes and Loggam took the long way through the woods home, he just wanted to be by himself for a while.

When he arrived home, he started writing a letter to Jenny. He knew he was going to see her in a week so he wouldn't bother mailing it. She was just the person whom he felt the closest too. He poured his heart out over how said he was losing his dad's hat. He realized it was just a hat, but for some reason knowing it was the one his dad always wore opened old wounds losing it. Loggam couldn't help but shed a few tears. He looked at the picture he had sitting on his nightstand. The picture was of Loggam as a baby, his mom and his dad, and of course, on the top of his dad's head, the hat. Loggam thought about what a difference life would have been had his dad still been alive. He didn't really want to talk to his mom about how Trent was bullying him and wished his dad were here to tell him what to do. Loggam decided he'd turn in early and just get a good night's sleep. He made plans with Eric tomorrow. They were going to spend the day just the two of them.

Over the next several days Loggam spent much of his time with the group of boys, particularly Eric. He'd been called many names from Trent and did his best to avoid him. Trent also spilled Loggam's soda, broke his compass, and kicked dirt at him all in the name of accidents. Trent was careful with his timing and made sure to do these things when none of the adults were around. Loggam wasn't a tattletale and decided he wasn't going to let Trent win by showing him it was getting to him. Besides, through all of this, his friendship with Eric blossomed and that made being there worth it. Loggam realized that the more he didn't react to Trent, the less the harassment. Trent was looking for feedback, he wanted to see that he was getting to him and Loggam just refused to provide that for him. Nothing could really get Loggam down now anyway because he knew Jenny was due to arrive the next day. He'd told Eric all about her, and couldn't wait for them to meet. He knew they'd get along well; he just wanted to keep Jenny away from Trent. Jenny was a tough cookie and didn't need any type of coddling from Loggam, but Loggam still felt it was his responsibility to protect her; it was how he was raised.

The day was finally here. Loggam sat on the step outside his house waiting for the Mallets to arrive. He knew they traditionally got there around 1:00 PM. He'd been sitting outside since eleven, hoping maybe they'd show early. Around one thirty, the camper pulled down the dirt road heading into Loggam's driveway, and he nearly exploded with excitement! Jenny was waving her hand ferociously in the window. Nearly could wait for the camper to stop, and the second the tires didn't move, the camper door flung open, and Jenny was down those steps as if she flew. She jumped into Loggam's awaiting arms and they held one another as tight as the both could. Judith came running out of the house and hugged both Mindy and Ken. They are watched as Loggam and Jenny still didn't let go of their embrace. Loggam took a step back and just admired his Jenny. She was becoming so beautiful, he thought. Her long, strawberry-blond hair against her pale skin, she had these big blue/green eyes and freckles sprinkled across her cheeks. Loggam quickly tried to get that thought from his mind. Jenny was his best friend. He was just kind of shocked to see how grown up she looked. Jenny also stared back at the changes in Loggam. Each one had lost that childlike look since they'd last seen one another. Ken and Mindy realized they'd have to be the ones to greet Loggam as his attention was 100 percent Jennyfied.

"Hello, Loggam. How are ya, son?" Ken asked.

"Mr. Mallet, I am sorry," he chuckled. "I just hadn't seen Jenny in so long. She looks so different to me. I am doing well, sir. It's so good to see you all."

Ken laughed and agreed that he too had changed in the year it had been since they'd seen one another last. They all went into Judith's modest little house and caught up.

Loggam and Jenny excused themselves, and he took her into his room to show her the letter he'd written to her. He told her all about Eric, his new friend, and Trent, his not-so-new friend. Jenny became protective of Loggam and wanted to be taken to Trent right away. She tightened her lights into a scowl and said, "If he messes with you, he messes with me."

Loggam couldn't help but smile because she was serious and one tough girl. A boy didn't in the least bit intimidate her. As a matter of fact, Loggam realized for Trent's safety, he should probably keep them apart. She wouldn't mind showing him just what she thought!

Later that night Judith ad Loggam joined the Mallets over at their campsite. They sat around a fire, and Loggam invited Eric who was due to show in anytime. When Eric walked up, he immediately noticed Jenny. He went straight up to her, almost completely ignoring Loggam and introduced himself. Jenny grinned and giggled as she'd noticed him taking a liking to her too. A new emotion came over Loggam, one he wasn't quite familiar with. All he knew was whatever this feeling was, he didn't much like it, and he felt like telling Eric he could leave all of a sudden. Jenny and Eric exchanged small talk while Loggam sorted out his emotions momentarily. He joined in the conversation and realized whatever he was feeling was crazy. Jenny was his best friend, and Eric was a good new friend to him too.

"Do you like scary stories Jenny?" Eric asked.

Jenny thought this was a strange question but answered Eric, "Yeah, I do kind of. I don't like scary movies though, just stories."

"Cool, at my camp right now, we have scary story night where each one of us tells the most terrifying story we know. It's really fun, would you two like to go and do that? They also have s'mores."

Loggam was a bit nervous as he knew that Trent would be there, but he also realized he couldn't stop fun because of Trent either. Jenny was excited to go, and after her parents gave the okay, the three started heading through woods toward the boy's campsite. Once they arrived, all the boys were sitting around the fire making their s'mores, and one of the boys held a flashlight under their chin highlighting their face.

Charlie was in the midst of telling his story when he yelled, "BAM!" and all the boys jumped up startled. Charlie laughed and wailed, "Got ya!" as the boys relaxed from their moment of alarm.

As Loggam, Jenny, and Eric walked up, the boys moved down to make room for them. Jenny could immediately tell which was Trent as he glared at all three of them, and she glared right back. Each made their introductions and got to know one another. Loggam was pleased that each boy (aside from Trent) was welcoming to her. Some of the boys had funny grins on their faces when they spoke to her. Jenny asked if she could go next, and Chad gladly grabbed the flashlight from Charlie and gave it to her. Jenny giggled and thanked him as she assumed her most frightening face and lit the flashlight under her chin.

"Once upon a time, there was a witch who lived in the woods among many townspeople. The folks feared the witch because it was said if you walked among the woods at night, you'd never return home again. One night, during the pouring rain, little Alice found herself lost in the woods. Every time she thought she found a trail, she just went deeper and deeper into the woods. She heard wolves howling and coyotes screeching. She had only a small flashlight that was growing dimmer and dimmer by the minute. She heard the sounds of feet behind her as she felt like someone was watching. She called out, 'Hello,' into the darkness, and she heard it echo through the darkness. She kept walking on a little faster now, and the footsteps continued at a faster pace. She heard an eerie sound of laughter in the wind. She cried and ran deeper into the darkness before tripping on a tree limb. A giant shadow stood above her, and she screamed! Alice was never to be heard from again, and it's been said the witch searches in the night for stray kids walking in the woods. The end."

All the boys acted tough but looked at the dark woods surrounding them. Jenny smiled, as she knew some of them were scared. "Anyone want to go in the woods for more firewood" Jenny asked.

Trent jumped up. "You're all scaredy-cats! You think I will get scared from a story some little girl tells?" Loggam rolled his eyes and looked at Jenny, he could tell she was paying no mind to Trent at all.

"Well, if you're not scared, why don't you go get the firewood then, Trent," Jenny stated.

"I will. Let's go, guys."

"Oh, you need your fleet to go along with you? Why don't you just go?"

Trent's face grew red, and he yelled, "Fine!" before storming off into the woods by himself.

After Trent returned five minutes later, he held one piece of firewood, and he threw it on the lit flames. Jenny and Loggam said their goodbyes and decided to head home for the night. The next day, they had plans, just the two of them.

Loggam showed up early to the Mallets' camper. He had a picnic basket and a backpack ready for their hike together. Jenny and Loggam had a place in the woods they considered their very own. It was a beautiful meadow that had wildflowers of every color and a creek that ran through it. They had found it a few years ago and made it their secret rendezvous spot ever since.

Together, they walked to their secret hideaway and marveled at the beauty when they arrived. Jenny was quick to pick as many wildflowers as she could as Loggam spread the blanket and pulled out the peanut-butter-and-jelly sandwiches her made for them. He also brought two yoo-hoos as they were Jenny's favorite.

The two sat and spoke about school and friends they both had. Loggam loved how animated Jenny would get when telling stories. Head to head they lay across the warm grass and ate up the sunshine.

Jenny popped up quickly and said, "Loggam, do you hear that sound?" Loggam listened for a few moments and only heard the trees shake in the breeze and birds chirping.

"There it was again," Jenny said. This time Loggam thought he did hear a faint sound. Loggam stood up and faced the direction he thought he heard it coming from. He closed his eyes and listened harder.

"I think I heard someone yelling for help!" Loggam exclaimed. "Let's go!"

The two ran as fast as they could toward the faint sound in the distance, as they grew closer the wailing grew louder. Loggam ran up the mountainside where he found bikes thrown across the ground and four boys from camp standing there looking terrified.

"What is happening? I heard yelling for help," Loggam asked.

Charlie started explaining the story to Loggam. "We were riding our bikes on the trail, and Ben told us to stay close by, on the trails we rode yesterday. Trent wanted to go farther, and we followed him up this path. We wanted to make a mount to launch our bikes from and see who had the coolest jump. Trent lost control of his bike and flew off the mountain. He's stuck hanging right over there."

With that, Loggam ran to the edge of the cliff and, sure enough, found Trent hanging on for dear life to roots and vines in the ground. "We tried to help him, but we're all afraid of heights, and he's too far down for us to grab. We sent Chad for help, but he's been gone for a while."

Loggam immediately jumped into action. He leaned over the cliff and starting talking to Trent. "Listen, Trent, we are going to get you out of there. You need to stay calm. Do you have a firm grip? See that tree beside your right hand?"

"Um, yeah."

"Okay, carefully grab that. It will support you better. Does anyone else have a belt on?" Each boy started removing his utility belts.

"Okay, this is what we are going to do, Charlie and Eric, you get on one side of me, and, Trevor and Pat, you get on this one. I'm going to use these two belts to loop around his back and secure him. You need to hang me over the cliff and each pair hold my legs. When I say pull, you hold on with all your life and drag me back up. Do you all understand? Jenny, if either team is struggling, just grab on and pull with them, okay?"

All the boys agreed and got into position. Loggam looked over the cliff. It was a long way down that ended with giant rocks and trees. He gathered his nerve and lay across the ground with his upper body hanging over the edge.

"Okay, guys. Grab my legs and start lowering me down slowly until you hear me say stop. Got that?"

"Yes, we understand."

Slowly, the boys lowered Loggam until his whole body was hanging over the cliff, and then when he was close enough to Trent, he yelled, "Stop!"

"Okay, Trent, listen carefully, do not let go of anything. I am going to loop this belt around your back and tighten it against your stomach. Then I'm going to use this second belt and do the same. I will be pulling you up from there, and when I tell the guys to pull, you're going to try to climb with your hands and feet up this mountain."

"I am too scared to let go, Loggam. I can't let go!" Trent cried out.

"You need to trust me, Trent. This will work, and if you fall, I fall. On the count of three, we are going to do this. Okay, boys, on the count of three, pull with all you got! Ready?"

"ONE! TWO! THREE!"

With that, the boys dug their feet into the dirt and pulled on Loggam's legs as hard as they could. Jenny noticed Eric needing help and grabbed on and started pulling. Loggam looped the belts around his chest and pulled as Trent clawed at the earth, trying to make his way up. After what felt like forever, Loggam was on solid ground and was able to use his legs to pull Trent the rest of the way. With a big thud, Trent was back on solid ground.

Each boy lay flat across the dirt, sweating and taking big gulps of air. No one spoke, and everyone just continued lying there. A few minutes later, Trent crawled over to Loggam and grabbed him into a bear hug and cried out his forever gratitude. His words were barely audible amongst his tears.

"I was so mean to you, Loggam. I did such bad things to you, and you risked your life for me. I am so sorry, Loggam. I'm just so sorry," Trent cried out. Loggam hugged him back and let him get it all out.

Just then, Chad was back with Ben, two other counselors, and a forest ranger. They ran up and inspected Trent to make sure he was okay. Aside from some cuts and bruises on his legs from experience, he was okay. The boys were all quick to speak over one another telling them the entire story and how Loggam was a hero and orchestrated the whole rescue. Loggam felt slightly uncomfortable accepting all this praise, and after he was assured everyone was all right, left with Jenny back to gather their things back at their hideaway.

Jenny couldn't take her eyes off Loggam. She stared at him in a different light than she ever had before. He bewildered her. Loggam tried to act as if he didn't notice because he wasn't able to contain his blushing. He was glad when they arrived back at their destination because he knew his cheeks were about as red as an apple. They gathered their things and decided to head home as they had a pretty epic day already.

During the walk back, Loggam was slightly saddened that the summer break was coming to a close. In two days, they'd have their summer festival at the park. He was so glad to have Jenny accompany him this year.

"Are you excited about the festival Jenny?"

"Oh yes. I can't wait to go together. I wonder if they will have any rides this year?"

"I don't know. I do hope so."

The following morning, Loggam heard a knock at his front door. He went over to answer it and found Trent standing on the other side.

"Hey, Loggam, do you think we can take a walk?"

"Yeah, sure. Let me just tell my mom I'm leaving." Loggam ran over to his mom and let her know and was out the door.

The beginning of their walk was silent. Loggam could tell Trent was thinking and trying to form his words.

"I will never be able to thank you enough for what you did for me. I wish I could say I would have been brave enough to do that for someone, but what makes me ever more shocking is that you did it for me. I was so horrible to you man, and you didn't even do anything to deserve the way I treated you. What made you help me?"

Loggam thought for a moment on how he wanted to answer that. "Well, you were in need of help, and I was there. Listen, Trent, I don't excuse the way you treated me, and I can only hope after all this, you'll think twice before bullying the new guy. I know that we are all only human and capable of making mistakes. Whether you were good to me or not, I couldn't let you hang there knowing I could do something; it's not my style."

"My other friends just stood there. They didn't know what to do."

"Yes, well, they were in shock and scared and just needed someone to take the lead. Without them, it wouldn't have worked. It was a team effort, Trent, and that's the way life should be."

Trent thought over Loggam's words and felt a sense of comfort speaking so freely with him. "I have three older brothers, and I am the youngest. All my life, they also picked on me and didn't include me in anything. Sometimes my parents made them, and when that happened, they were especially mean to me. I remember this one time, they all started shooting me with their paintball guns. I had thought for the first time they wanted to me hang out with them, but they were just making fun of me. They always say I am a klutz and that I am annoying. For once, I just wanted them to accept me for who I was. I guess that's why sometimes with my friends, I get bossy. It's the only time I feel like my voice matters."

Loggam started to make sense of why Trent was the way he was and why he bullied others. "I'm sorry your brothers treat you that way. I wouldn't really understand what's that's like. Being an only child, I always wanted siblings. I actually always wanted a baby sister, and after what you've told me about brothers, maybe that's better!"

Both boys chuckled and then Trent stopped walking suddenly and reached into his backpack. Loggam's eyes grew wild when Trent pulled out his dad's John Deere hat.

"I am so sorry for taking this, Loggam. I have no excuses, and I was a jerk. I hope you can forgive me for everything I said and did to you and for taking this hat. It was so wrong of me. This experience has taught me a lot about who I want to be and who I don't want to be."

Loggam stared at the hat, and his eyes grew watery. He didn't think he'd ever see it again. He placed the hat on his head and smiled back at Trent. "Yes, I could be mad at you and hold a grudge, but what good will that do me? You have said you're sorry, and I can see that you are. You also have learned that treating people as your brothers treat you doesn't feel good. I do forgive you, Trent, and I hope we can be friends."

"Not just friends, Loggam. You will always be one of my best friends," Trent said with tears in his eyes. The boys hugged one more time, shook hands, and started walking back while talking about the summer festival.

It had finally arrived: the night of the festival. Loggam couldn't have been more excited. Loggam and Jenny had plans to meet Eric, Charlie, and Trent there by the popcorn stands. Jenny waited for Loggam outside his house, and when he came out the door, they were off. The festivities seemed even bigger this year with a large outcome of people. The trees were all twinkling with different-colored lights, the firepit was massive, and Loggam couldn't even count how many food vendors and candy vendors were there. They had their choice of many games to play. Loggam went right up to the first one he saw: he had to throw the rings around the glass bottle. The first two he missed, but the third was a perfect lasso, and he won Jenny a big green teddy bear. They continued walking trying not to be distracted by any more games and found Eric, Charlie, and Trent waiting by the popcorn machine.

"Hey, guys! This is great, isn't it?" Loggam exclaimed.

"Oh yeah, it is," Trent said. Trent walked over to Loggam and said, "We gotta go do the potato sack race, and we will totally rule that contest."

"Let's do it!"

The two boys each entered the same giant potato sack, and when the bell rang, had to get across the field as fast as they could. Eric and Charlie were beside them and other boys front the camp also were involved in the race. The bell rang and they were off! A few groups fell right at first hop whereas others went fast. Loggam and Trent worked together and made it to the finish line first. That had become the theme of the night as they had also won the one-legged bucket contest together. Mrs. Brown, Loggam's teacher, awarded him the golden medal made out of chocolate after he won tug-of-war. Hours passed, and they played every game they could get their hands on and ate as much junk food as their stomachs allowed!

Loggam looked at all his friends and felt very thankful he had them. He looked over at Trent and thought even with the toughest exterior, sometimes, you will find the dearest of friends if you just look beneath the surface and maintain faith in people. He cherished each and every one of his friends old and new, and they had a magical summer night. This summer was one he'd remember for a very long time.

Part Four

Love of a Lifetime

It was finally almost complete. One of the most important projects Loggam was working on. He'd followed a well thought-out road map to get here, and the time is almost up. He reached into the back pocket of his old Wrangler jeans and pulled out the drawing he'd meticulously studied for years and years. It was a drawing done by a twelve-year-old Jenny, and it was of her dream home.

He remembered the summer together when she sat and drew it up. She spent hours in front of that paper, lifting it and studying it for a moment before putting it down and adding more details. He'd never seen her so focused before. She had a variety of colored pencils, markers, and even a ruler. It was a beautiful two-story home with sky blue shutters and a pale yellow paint. The house had large windows throughout it to exploit the sunshine as much as possible. Jenny always talked about having a grand staircase, and Loggam paid special attention to ensure he met every detail of her imagination. He didn't furnish the house because he knew that she would have enjoyed the pleasure of doing that, however, he did build her massive bookshelves for her large assortment of books. Each day, he was involved in the process of building Jenny's dream home alongside the construction crew. On the final days, he put the finishing touches on the landscaping around the property. Jenny loved flowers and Japanese maple trees the most, so Loggam personally planted them. The wraparound porch in the front of the house was a sight to behold with a swing, handmade Adirondack chairs, and the most breathtaking view of the mountains.

A year back, Loggam purchased forty acres of property right beside Red Fir State Park. Jenny was still living at home with her family while she finished her degree. Later this month, Jenny is graduating college and set to move to Alabama shortly after. Jenny and Loggam had known one another from when they were both children and, throughout their lives, stayed the very best of friends.

During one of her many visits when she was sixteen, Loggam took her to their secret hideaway in the meadow and confessed he liked her much more than a friend. Jenny couldn't have been happier with Loggam's confession and proclaimed that she felt the same. They shared their first kiss sitting under a blanket of stars. The two started as best friends and transitioned into a beautiful young love. Though they had known one another for many years, it was like learning one another through brand new eyes. They couldn't stand being apart and spent much of their time writing or talking on the phone. They'd spend hours talking about everything and nothing at the same time just to have the opportunity to hear one another's voices. They'd made plans for the future and shared their deepest hopes and dreams. Each vacation, they stuck like magnets to one another. It wasn't a surprise to Judith, Loggam's mother, or Jenny's parents that they'd fallen in love, as it was such a deep obvious connection they had since they were children. As hard as it was, both Loggam and Jenny knew that she had to complete school and wait until they both were older before any moving arrangements would be made. They both cherished the times they had during their visits and enjoyed any form of communication they'd have until they could be together.

Loggam lifted her drawing in the air against the house in the background and smiled with sweet satisfaction. It was complete. Each element of the drawing and some added embellishments were finished. Jenny had been kept in the dark that Loggam was doing this; she hadn't even known he bought all the property. Now, he just had to sit back and wait until Jenny arrived to show her his surprise. He had the next phase of his plan to work on.

The next part of Loggam's plan had to wait until Jenny arrived in two days. He had the list of items he'd need and was just counting down the days. When the day came to execute his plan, he jumped out of bed at first light. Behind the new home he'd built, Loggam used stakes in the ground, creating a pathway from the backyard to their hideaway where they shared their first kiss and a vast amount of memories. Now, he removed each stake as he went and put in two lanterns on each side every two feet. When he reached the hideaway, he walked back toward his house stretching rope lighting on each side of the path he made. Next, he had to go into town and pick up the ring he bought. He had to have it sized appropriately to Jenny's slender finger. The ring was stunning; it was a vintage-inspired ring with a yellow gold band and a giant sapphire surrounded by diamond clusters. Jenny always loved sapphires because they symbolized wisdom and serenity. She said staring into its beauty always calmed her mind. He couldn't wait to give it to her, his excitement was buzzing through the air.

Just one more day, Loggam thought. After picking up the ring Loggam went to Superior Fireworks where he purchased the Excalibur artillery shell kit and Sheller kit which was a package that had wave shells, chrysanthemums, and willows. These were top-selling, professional-grade fireworks. Loggam wanted to make this night one they'd both remember forever. He knew he was about to propose to a hopeless romantic, and he'd give her the best he could conjure up.

The next day he set up all the fireworks in a part of his property that was the closest to their meadow. He had a friend of his all set to detonate the fireworks at 9:00 PM exactly. They would be able to have a clear view of them from the meadow. Loggam covered trees with white twinkle lights and had candles and lanterns hanging from the limbs in smoked glass bowls. He bought a white sheer canopy and hung it from the tree. The fabric cascaded over the blanket he had draped across the ground. He had pillar candles surrounding the blanket and a picnic basket that he'd fill with takeout from her favorite Italian restaurant. He was going to get chicken Parmesan, and for her, it had to be eggplant Parmesan. He'd have fresh, warm bread, a salad, and pumpkin cheesecake for dessert. He also brought a red wine. The restaurant was instructed to have the food ready by 6:00 PM.

Loggam was ready to go and his heart was pounding. He was so excited to see his Jenny; it felt like it had been so long. She told him she would meet him at their hideaway at six thirty that night. Loggam ran home and changed into a collared polo shirt and a pair of clean, dark-blue jeans. He had very few that didn't have holes or dirt stains worn into them. He checked himself over in the mirror and gave himself a little pep talk. He decided he still had some time so he'd go visit his mother, Judith.

Upon arriving at his mother's, he found her sitting outside with a book in one hand and a tall glass of sweet tea in the other.

"Hello, son. You look so handsome. Are all your plans set for tonight?" Judith asked in excitement.

"Yup, all set. Now, I just hope she says yes."

"Sweetheart, I knew that girl was your destiny when you two were kids. I have no doubt in my mind she will say yes. I am so proud of you, Loggam. You have always been such a virtuous man; I wish your father were here to see you now. But I know he is with us both and is equally just as gratified with the man you've become. Now, you be confident tonight and speak from your heart. That's how your father proposed to me; he didn't even have a ring yet, and he said his heart couldn't stand another minute without turning me into his bride. We were standing right outside of a movie theater when he pulled me out of line and dropped down to one knee! Oh, it was splendid. The crowd erupted in cheer and merriment for us." Judith looked off into the distance with a sweet smile on her face. She was captured by a memory that struck the cords of her heart. Loggam watched his mother and hoped that Jenny loved him the way his mother loved his dad.

Almost as if she was reading his mind Judith said, "She does, you know. She loves you like that."

Loggam was a bit taken back that his mother seemed to know exactly what he'd been thinking. He smiled and hugged his mother tight.

Loggam picked up the food at exactly 6:00 PM and started heading toward his hideaway. During his walk, he grabbed ample handfuls of loose change and scattered it through the busier parts of the park. This had become one of his favorite things to do.

As he passed the firepit, he scattered even more because this area held the thickest population of kids. When he arrived at his meadow, he put his belongings down and organized them into their appropriate place. He followed the trail he made through the woods, scattering rose petals, carnation petals, and some of the colorful wildflowers along the path he'd made. Once he returned, he set up the tent he brought for their night beneath the stars. Once that was finished, he lit the candles and lanterns and laid across the blanket and looked to the sky. First, he thanked the heavens for the beautiful weather they were having, for being almost summer, it was still reasonably comfortable. The skies were blue with giant marshmallow clouds, and the warm breeze was relaxing. Loggam said a little prayer of gratitude for all that he had and all that should come. He heard the crunching sounds of footsteps in the distance. He stood up and grabbed the wildflower bouquet he picked for Jenny, and there she was.

She was a vision, he thought. She wore a white sundress with pink flowers across the bodice. Her pale skin sparkled against the sunlight; her long blond hair was curled at the bottom. Her eyes were brilliantly blue with specks of green.

She completely dazzled me, Loggam thought. He ran toward her and scooped her up into his arms. They held one another in the tightest embrace. He spun her in circles in his arms and they both laughed happily. He slowly dropped her feet back to the ground as he ran his hands down her soft arms until their fingers locked together. Their eyes sealed on one another and he slowly bent in for a soft kiss.

"You look so beautiful, Jenny. I have missed you so much!"

"Thank you, Loggam," Jenny said while blushing. "I have missed you too."

Jenny marveled at her surroundings. "I can't believe you did this all. Loggam, it's simply breathtaking."

"This is only the beginning, Jenny. I wanted to make your first night living in Alabama special and commemorative. It's been so long since we camped out at our spot. I hope you still wanted to do that?"

"Oh yes, I'd love to. I'm finally here to stay! I don't have any of my things yet; my parents will be coming this weekend with their camper packed full!"

Jenny couldn't take her eyes off each and every detail. Even though it was still light out, the candles sparkled against the rays of sun shining through the trees. The flowers were in full bloom and covered almost every inch of their meadow.

"I don't want your food to get cold. Please join me." Loggam pointed to the blanket that had the food set up. It was insulated in the basket to keep warm.

"That smells delicious" Jenny said.

"I went with your favorite. wine?"

"Yes, please. Is that cheesecake?"

"Pumpkin cheesecake to be exact."

Both Jenny and Loggam savored each morsel of their food and caught up on small talk while not taking their eyes of one another for a second.

As the time passed, the sun started to set and the twilight glow set against the mountains was simply exquisite. Jenny laid against Loggam's arms as she drank in both her wine and the beauty of her surroundings. As the darkness approached, the trees lit up brilliantly with their twinkle lights, and the candles and lanterns created a romantic ambiance. Loggam almost forgot the time, as he sometimes did when Jenny was around. It was moments away from the first set of fireworks his buddy would be setting off.

"Jenny, I have a surprise for you. Don't be startled, as it might be a little loud momentarily."

Jenny looked at Loggam with a dumbfounded expression. Loggam turned her body toward the direction that would have the best visibility.

"What are we looking—"

Before Jenny could finish her sentence, the sky exploded with light. Bright blues, greens, reds, pinks took over the sky. Jenny jumped and then erupted with laughter and wonderment. They watched as some fizzled while other crackled and boomed. The finale seemed like it must have been done by more than one person because there wasn't a piece of sky that hadn't burst with colors.

"*Wow!*" Jenny mouthed to Loggam. He smiled deep and proud, receiving the exact reaction he hoped for.

After the show ended, Loggam built a fire for the two of them. It was time to trade in the wine glasses for mugs. Jenny was a stickler for hot cocoa and marshmallows regardless of the season. It had become a nighttime ritual when they were together. As they sat around the fire, Jenny noticed lights in the woods.

"Loggam, what are those lights over there for?"

"Oh, well, that's the last part of your surprise. I hope you don't mind waking up early, right before dawn?"

"Not at all, I love the woods the most at first light. Can you give me a hint at what we will be doing?" Jenny asked with a clever little grin. Loggam smiled back at her and ran his fingers across his lips signifying his lips were locked and sealed.

After finishing their cocoa, they went over to the blanket and lay across it looking up at the stars. The night was particularly clear with not a cloud in sight. The stars shined brilliantly against the dark sky.

"This, Loggam, this is what I have dreamed about. Lying here with you just like this."

"I've counted down the days until I had you back in my arms, Jenny. I'm at my happiest when I have you by my side," he said as he kissed her forehead. Although Loggam had a tent all ready to go, both Jenny and him fell asleep laying across the blanket wrapped in one another's grasp.

Loggam woke to little vibrations from his wristwatch. With a big yawn and stretch, he looked down at Jenny who was still fast asleep cuddled up against his belly. He almost hated disturbing her when she looked so peaceful. He took a few minutes just to comb the hair off her face and admire the soft details of her beautiful expression. Although her wanted to stay like this forever, he knew the timing had to be just perfect so he gently kissed her cheek to wake her up. Her eyes slowly opened and met his and she smiled.

"Is it time for my next surprise?" she asked.

Loggam hugged her tight and lifted them both to their feet. "Yes, it is," he replied.

He grabbed her hand and directed her toward the path. It glowed charmingly against the veil of darkness. As they walked along the path the sky slowly turned from dark blue to gray, and Jenny was beginning to see her surroundings. She noticed the petals she was walking on and kneeled down to them, she lifted them into a big pile and tossed them into the air. She threw her head back and laughed as they came cascading down all around her. As they continued down the path, Jenny noticed a clearing ahead.

"Now, Jenny, may I have your permission to blindfold you the rest of the way?" he asked with a smirk.

Jenny giggled and gave her blessing. "Don't let me fall," she said.

"Never," Loggam replied. He secured the blindfold across her face and held onto her close so she wouldn't trip on anything within their path. As he stepped onto his property, they were now in the backyard of the house. He walked her to the front and arranged her so her back was to the house. When he removed the blindfold, she opened her eyes to woods in front of her. Loggam's heart was pounding so fast, he felt himself starting to sweat. This was the moment he'd spend years planning for.

Suddenly, as if time had stopped, Loggam felt this strong sensation. His skin had goose bumps and his hair stood up on his arms. The scent in the air was strongly reminiscent of his father's cologne. Loggam had the strongest sense that his father was standing there with him. So much so that it actually brought tears to his eyes. This feeling filled him with so much comfort and strength; it was just what he needed.

Jenny noticed the subtle change in Loggam. "Are you all right?"

"Yes, I am more than all right. I am the happiest I've ever been." Loggam grabbed Jenny's hands and continued on. "I still remember the first time I saw you, Jenny, wearing a white sundress standing on the steps of your parents' camper. I think it was in that moment, my life was plotted out for me. My destiny was decided. I've waited a long time for this very moment."

With that Loggam slowly dropped down to kneel before her. She quickly covered her shocked expression. "Jenny, I love you with all of my heart, would you do me the finest honor and marry me?"

Jenny couldn't control the outpour of tears that rushed down her face. She took Loggam hands and lifted him to his full height as she jumped into his arms wailing yes. Together, they clung to one another, both with tears of love and joy in their eyes.

Loggam reached into his pocket and handed her the drawing she had done of her dream home. She looked at it slightly bewildered as to why he gave this to her. As she stared at it, he turned her around.

As she looked up she almost fainted. He quickly stood behind her to steady her. Jenny was speechless.

"I...I... You... How?" Jenny couldn't even form the words. Every single detail of her drawing came to life before her very eyes. She pinched her own arm to make sure this wasn't all a dream. Tears of joy just kept rolling down her cheeks.

"Loggam, I can't believe you did this for me. I remember when I drew this house as a little girl. I was still very sick at the time. I never thought the day would come that I would even be around to have my own place let alone my dream home."

Jenny grabbed Loggam and squeezed him into an embrace. The beauty of this man would never cease to amaze her. Loggam took Jenny's hands and walked her toward the house.

"Let's head inside," Loggam said with a big grin spread across his cheeks. Nothing satisfied him more than bringing happiness to his Jenny. Giving this gift was just as rewarding for him as receiving it.

Hand in hand, they walked into the house and Jenny's eyes were immediately drawn to the beautifully handcrafted staircase. She ran her hands over the railing and marveled at the handiwork. At the top of the staircase was something square and small. She looked over at Loggam, and he just wore a grin. She climbed up the steps and found a velvet box awaiting her. She lifted it slowly as if it could crumble in her fingers any moment. Loggam met her at the top of the staircase. He sat her down at the top and kneeled down once again below her.

He took the box from her and opened it presenting the lovely sapphire and diamond ring.

Jenny covered her mouth and cried. "Oh, Loggam! It's breathtaking! It's exquisite!"

Loggam removed the ring from it velvet case and slid it on her finger. "When I had seen this ring, I knew it was you. It gives me all the pride a man could possibly have that you wear it. You've always been the girl for me, Jenny, and it makes me the happiest man in the world that you said yes."

With those words, Jenny jumped into his arms and held him as tight as she could. She felt so safe, so complete; nothing could compare to the happiness of this very moment in time.

"Now," Loggam said. "Let's check out the rest of this house!"

With that, she ran down the staircase and through the kitchen like a child who was positively giddy over each detail Loggam was sure to include. Every few moments she'd stare down at her magnificent ring and just smile. The sunshine was pooling into the home as it rose in the early morning sky. Its rays splashed and danced across each surface within the home.

"I love all this sunshine coming in," Jenny said.

After a long stretch of going through each and every corner of the house, Loggam and Jenny sat down in the middle of the living-room floor. Her eyes wandered all about as she was decorating in her head what would go where.

"This has been the best weekend of my life," Jenny said.

"Mine too, Jenny."

She lifted her hand in front of them both. "Mrs. Jenny Maggel," she said. Loggam smiled so hard his face almost hurt.

Over the duration of the next few weeks, both Loggam and Jenny stayed very busy, furnishing their new home and making wedding plans. Jenny's family decided to stay for the month to help with the planning and getting them settled into their home. Jenny always dreamed of having a fall wedding. The thought of being surrounded by orange maple trees, scarlet dogwoods, and golden hickories all gleaming with glittering yellow and gold colors just enthralled her. Fall was that time of the year when the summer surrendered its blanket of green and traded it in for a quilt of color. Being that autumn, too, was Loggam's favorite season, he was happy to comply. They both wanted a simple wedding surrounded by family and some close friends. They felt they'd have enough time to plan over the summer. Plus, that would give them the time they needed to finish any last details of their house.

The next few months had been tremendously busy for both Loggam and Jenny. They just about finished decorating and filling their new home, and the wedding plans were almost done too. Some small final touches were all that was left to prepare for. Jenny was excited that she had landed the job she had wanted for many years. Ever since she was a small child and battled cancer herself, she had made it her life's purpose to help other children going through what she had. She had finished her RN school back home before moving to Alabama and the additional training and testing in the past few months here. She applied to the same hospital she was treated at when she was little. She was so thrilled to work under Dr. Chen, who is the chief of staff and also happens to be the man responsible for saving her life. During the days Jenny was at work, Loggam was occupied building his wedding present for Jenny.

Gathering his bricks, stone, wood, and steel Loggam gave him quiet the ambitious masonry project. He was building stables on his property. He knew both he and Jenny always wanted farm animals, particularly horses, one day. Loggam loved working with his hands out in fresh clean Alabama air. Nothing made him happier than creating something from nothing and mostly fulfilling his sweetheart's dream.

The weeks passed rather quickly, and Loggam and Jenny's wedding was approaching. Friends and acquaintances had started to both fly in and drive in to be in attendance. Red Fir State Park had full occupancy. Loggam was so touched to see how many friends he's made over the years had shown up. As Loggam was walking through the campground, dropping coins off as we went, he felt a tap on his shoulder.

"Well, if this wasn't a huge surprise!" Loggam exclaimed. Trent, a face from Loggam's teenage years, stared back at him. Trent and

Loggam didn't make the best start of things back when they were kids. In fact, to be frank, Trent was a bully. A bully that had his eyes opened by one Loggam Maggel, and now here they were, many moons later, friends. "I can't believe you made it, I am so happy to see you. Jenny is going to be so excited too!"

"I couldn't miss the wedding of you two. Luckily, you happened to plan it while I am on leave."

"How is the army life? Where are you stationed now?"

"I am in Fort Campbell in Kentucky. I just returned from a year in Afghanistan. It's nice to have a little R and R with old friends. I brought Eric and Matt with me too. They're going to come by later."

"Wow, really? Gosh, it will be great to see them both too. Man, it's good to see you, friend. And thank you. Thank you for your service to our country and for coming." Loggam grabbed Trent's hand and shook it hard and grabbed him in for a hug. He was so happy to see his friend again after so many years.

The day continued to be filled with reunions as Loggam walked through the campground. He was stopped by many and never was without a smile. His heart was touched by the sheer amount of people who came to be there for the wedding. Jenny and him had wanted to keep things informal and sent out invites and evites to all the campers on the registry they knew well from Red Fir. They also had invited campers who happened to be visiting this weekend. Loggam had hired a local company to cater and make all the food. Because they didn't have a traditional RSVP list, they only had an idea of the high numbers of guests. The caterers were making Alabama's finest crawfish pie, fried green tomatoes, collard greens, baked grits, pulled pork, fried chicken, and many decadent desserts. They had an ample amount of folding chairs, picnic tables, plus large long logs that kids could sit on. Jenny had custom-ordered her wedding cake. It was a rustic-themed cake with fall colored leaves scattered throughout the cake and fake twigs going up the icing. It fit her taste and Loggam's to the T!

Later that night, many of the guests who had just arrived as well as the locals decided to meet at Skully Lake. It was an informal wedding rehearsal and get-together. Loggam built a big fire as the nights had started to cool off a bit. He brought several bags of marshmallows and hot cocoa. He also brought disposable cups and plenty of hot dogs and hamburger to grill. Judith, Loggam's mother, brought different salads and chips with dip. They made sure they had enough to go around. As more people gathered, the area around Skully Lake filled up. Jenny was excited to see all their guests and relatives from back home. It was a wonderful evening filled with many reunions and laughter.

Later that night, Loggam kissed his Jenny good night and went to stay at his mom's house. Jenny had her family staying with her as it's bad luck for the groom to see the bride the night before the wedding. Jenny felt like a kid again surrounded by all her female cousins. They went through old photos and laughed over old memories. She was having the time of her life. She knew she needed a good night's sleep but hardly wanted the night to end! When she finally lay in bed that night, she thanked God for all the blessings in her life. She thanked God for her family and for Loggam.

It is finally here: my wedding day, Loggam thought. *How did I get so lucky to have found Jenny? She is such an incredible woman.*

"Loggam you in there?" Judith came walking into the room, calling out.

"Yes, Mom. Right here."

"You look so handsome." Judith stared at her son with joy in her expression. He was dressed up so nicely in a shirt and tie with beige dress pants.

"I'm so excited, Mom. I just wish dad was here too."

Judith wiped the tears building in her eyes and sniffled. "I know, hunny. Me too. But we both know that he is here with us. Close your eyes and feel him here."

"I love you, Mom."

"And I love you too, my boy."

"Hey, Mom. You look beautiful too."

Judith smiled and nodded, grabbed Loggam's hand as they walked out of the room. Together, they left and headed for the church.

It was a tiny little church down a dirt road about twenty-five minutes from where they lived. Since it was such a small place, only family and close friends would join for the ceremony, and they'd meet after at the reception at Red Fir. Each pew had beautiful wildflowers attached along the aisle. Candles adorned they altar where they'd be standing. Both Loggam's small family, which consisted of some distant cousins on his dad's side, and Jenny's bigger family congregated into the church. Loggam walked up to the pastor and shook his hand. Moments later, the organs started playing the traditional wedding march, and descending almost like an angel was Jenny in the doorway of the church gripping her father's arm. Loggam felt almost weak in the knees when he first saw her. His vision slightly distorted due to the tears in his eyes.

She wore a Chantilly lace ivory dress with a long veil. Her beautiful blond hair was cascading down in tendrils with pearls hair clips. She looked positively exquisite.

"Don't let me fall, Dad," Jenny said nervously as she made her first steps down the aisle.

"Never," he responded and nudged a little closer to her.

Loggam and Jenny's eyes locked and throughout the ceremony; they didn't look away from one another. They exchanged their handwritten vows to one another and then the rings. They sealed their union with a kiss before the pastor announced, "May I present to you, Mr. and Mrs. Loggam Maggel!"

Tears were shed, merriment broke out among the small gathering. Many hugs and kisses were exchanged as Jenny and Loggam just basked in the glory of these unforgettable moments.

The gathering made their way over to the reception at Red Fir whereas Loggam and Jenny stayed behind to take some of their photographs together. When they arrived, they were announced by the band and entered the reception area to a large crowd of applause and laughter. Both Loggam and Jenny were awestruck by how many of their friends and family were there. They felt deeply touched that they had this much love and support in their lives. The band had announced for them to share their first dance to which they danced to Tracy Byrd's "The Keeper of the Stars." Each time the chorus played, singing "I tip my hat," Loggam would remove his hat and tip it to the skies above, and Jenny giggled.

The next song was a fast one, "The Devil Went Down to Georgia." This one created lots of foot stomping and laughter. Some of the couples started to square dance, so Judith grabbed hold of the Deegan family and joined in.

After the cake was cut and passed around, Loggam requested that Jenny join him for a quick exploration of their property. This wasn't too far of a walk from Red Fir. As they approached their property, Loggam grinned big knowing this was the perfect gift.

"I have a wedding present for you, Jenny."

"Oh, do you? I also have one for you too."

"I'd gotten farther along in the stables then I had let on."

Jenny stated smiling from ear to ear. "Had you?" she said giggling.

Loggam ran a little way ahead of her, opened the stable door, and within a few moments, came out leading a magnificent golden palomino horse. Jenny's eyes lit up like fireworks. Since her childhood, she'd dreamed of having a palomino just like her grandpa did.

"Oh, Loggam. She's breathtaking." Jenny went over and started petting the horse. She couldn't take her eyes off her splendor.

"I'm going to name her Duchess, just like my granddad's. This is by far the best gift I've ever received." Jenny grabbed Loggam into an embrace and hugged him with all her strength.

"Let me grab mine. His name is Trigger." Loggam went back to the stables and lead out a black and white pinto. Jenny once again marveled at the gorgeous creature. "Now we can go riding together as we've always talked about."

The horses grazed among the grass as Loggam and Jenny relished the moment together with them.

"Hey, Jenny what do you say we take them back to Red Fir?" Loggam asked, wearing a sideways grin.

"In my wedding dress?" Jenny said, laughing.

"Sure, I'll help you get on her."

"Okay, let's do it!"

After Loggam put the saddles on he'd bought on each horse, he helped Jenny carefully climb onto Duchess's back. He then spread her dress so it wouldn't drag or tear. He then jumped up on Trigger and they started off.

When they arrived, everyone admired at the beauty of both horses. Loggam tied them to the tree, and they happily grazed on the lush green grass. Judith and both Jenny's parents had already known about them. Jenny walked over to the food and grabbed a few apples for Duchess and Trigger. She had some of the children in attendance feed them to the horses.

The evening colors splashed across the sky as the glittering twinkle lights and candles' light started to express themselves through soft hues. Everyone was enthralled with pleasure as the food was delectable, the dancing was invigorating and the energy was abundantly blissful. Jenny and Loggam couldn't have dreamed of a better wedding day. They had locked eyes onto one another and held one another's hands in a firm grasp.

"Happiness is forever ours, my love. It's always there for the taking," Loggam said as he kissed Jenny's forehead as they went on celebrating their picturesque wedding day.

Part Five

Tarzan

Loggam and Jenny had settled happily into married life. They had full and fulfilling schedules that kept them busy. It made the quiet times that much more gratifying. Jenny worked long shifts at the hospital in the pediatric oncology department as a registered nurse. Each child she attended held a very special place in her heart. She understood more than most what they were feeling both physically and emotionally. She had a special way, unlike most of the other staff, when it came to facilitating their special needs. Even on her days off, Jenny would visit the children.

Loggam spent much of his time building more stables and barns for the farm they were creating. Over the past few months, he'd made much progress with his construction. They even adopted rescue animals already to fill some of the open space. They adopted three cats named Milo, Cinnamon, and George. They adopted a German shepherd who used to work on the police force. He was very well-trained and sweet-natured. They used the name he was already familiar with, Fred. They also got chickens, goats, bunny rabbits, pigs, and a few dairy cows. Let's just say the new additions kept Loggam and Jenny very busy!

Both Jenny and Loggam loved working on their farm. The final destination was to open a petting zoo for the children in the area. They wanted to have a place to teach children about animals and how to care for them. Loggam worked tirelessly on trying to finish the farm so they could open it to the public by the following month and bring some of the kids from the hospital. Loggam was fortunate to have help from his friend, Brandon, who lived a few miles away. Judith, Loggam's mom, would come often to tend to the animals. She loved spending all her time with them. Fred had loved it whenever Judith came over because she always carried a pocketful of dog treats. Frankly, all the animals enjoyed her constant visits because she had pockets full of treats for all of them. Loggam and Jenny laughed when she'd show up with all her pockets and purse filled to the brim!

Loggam decided he would take a little break from construction and take a long walk through Red Fir State Park. He drove into town first to withdraw one hundred dollars in loose change. He started his walk by Skully Lake, a popular spot for the campers to walk too. It was always full of children in this area. The smell of smoke from a campfire clung to the air. The sounds of birds chirping, distant children's laughter, and crunching from the twigs and leaves below your feet filled the atmosphere. Loggam reached deep into his pockets and began to scatter that loose change. The sun's rays caught the reflective surface of the change and shined vividly against the dirt. Loggam kept walking further, deciding he wanted to really stretch his limbs for a while. After some time, he'd progressed deep into the woodlands. He'd never get lost out here, as he knew these forests like that back of his hand. Others, however, wouldn't share in that ability. In the distance, Loggam could have sworn he saw a little shape.

Could it be all the way out here? Loggam thought to himself. *No, no child would be this far, especially by themselves.*

Loggam quickened his pace and started in on where he saw the shape. As he got closer, to his complete surprise, a young boy stood before him. Loggam was immediately taken by the boy's appearance. He had dirt marks all over his face, his clothes were dirty and torn, and his coloring was pale as a ghost. It had looked as if this young man had been out here for some time.

"Hello, son. Are you all right?"

The boy looked timidly at Loggam and backed up a step. He didn't reply to Loggam and looked alarmed.

"No need to be frightened. My name is Loggam. I live close by and was just taking a walk. Are you lost? Are you parents campers here?"

The young boy cleared his throat and finally spoke up. "No. No mama or papa. I live here all by myself, like Tarzan," he said with a hint of resilience.

Loggam smirked a bit but tried not to laugh as it might upset the boy. "Well, then. What do I call you then? I suppose your name isn't Tarzan now, is it?"

The boy grabbed his chin and looked into the air as he thought about his response. "How about you just call me Tarzan."

Loggam nodded. "Tarzan it is. Well, Tarzan, you look like you might be hungry. Would you like to walk back with me to get some food?"

His eyes immediately perked up at the word *food*. "Sure, I can eat."

Together Loggam and the boy walked back toward Loggam's property. Loggam tried asking more questions to find out more information but didn't get very far.

When they arrived back Loggam saw Jennie's car in the drive-way. "Hey, ah, Tarzan, I'd like you to meet my wife, Jenny, but would you like to wash up first before we eat something?"

The boy looked at his filthy hands and nodded.

"The bathroom is right in here. Here is the soap and fresh towels." Loggam wanted a chance to fill Jenny in while Tarzan was occupied.

Jenny was deeply concerned just as Loggam was but agreed, first things first, get the young man fed and cleaned up, then they'd both try to get more information out of him. Tarzan walked out of the bathroom and over to Loggam who was standing with Jenny.

"Hello, Tarzan, is it? My name is Jenny. It's nice to meet you. You must be hungry. What is something you really like to eat?"

The boy's eyes lit up with wonder and quickly yelled out, "Pizza! Pizza is my favorite thing. I've had it only when I was really, really good. Well, that's when the others didn't steal mine." His face became solemn as he recalled this memory. Jenny and Loggam tried to gauge where he might be from based on this tidbit of information.

Jenny knelt down in front of the boy and said, "What do you say we order you a pizza then? Maybe you can tell us more about where you're from?"

"I kinda don't wanna talk about it. I ain't going back. My home is the woods now," he said with a saddened expression. Loggam didn't wanna push too hard and have the boy run off. They'd get to the bottom of where he was from, but they felt their current task was to keep him safe.

After Jenny ordered the pizza, she went through old clothes they had. Of course, they didn't have anything small enough to accommodate an eight-year-old, but she found a pair of scrubs she was able to cut and clip smaller.

"Tarzan, I am sure you would like to get out of those dirty clothes. Why don't we take a quick bath while we wait for Loggam to pick up the pizza?"

The boy looked happy to get out of the clothes, even he was aware of their unpleasant scent. Jenny filled the tub with bubble bath for him and put fresh towels on the counter.

"Can you stay close, Ms. Jenny?"

"Of course, I can. I will sit right here with my book so if you need me, I'll be right here."

The boy smiled and quickly jumped into the bubbles. He splashed around and played acting as if the shampoo bottle was a rocket. Jenny read her book but couldn't help but smile.

He was just this little boy, she thought. *Whatever was he doing all by himself?* She would get to the bottom of this, she had to, and someone could be out there looking for him.

Loggam left the house a little early to pick up the pizza to stop by the local police station and meet with his friend, Brandon. He'd seen him earlier in that day when he helped with the farm. He'd already called him from home, and he was hoping by the time he arrived, Brandon might have found a missing person ad for Tarzan.

"So, did you have any luck?"

"Nothing has come up in this county that meets his description. I've also called some of my local contacts to see if they heard of a missing child. Nothing."

"Well, keep on the lookout for anything. I will continue to try to find out more from him. He can stay with us until we find something out." Brandon said he was going to check more channels to see if he could dig anything up.

When Loggam arrived home with the pizza, Tarzan almost looked like a different kid. Without the dirt, Loggam could make out his sandy-blond hair and the dimples on his cheeks. His deep blue eyes looked longingly at the pizza box. Loggam quickly dropped it down on the dining room table, grabbed some plates, and told him to dig in. Tarzan was practically drooling over the pizza, but still, he waited to take a slice. Jenny and Loggam looked at one another, taking notice of this.

"Let me grab that slice for you." Jenny placed the slice on his plate, and now his eyes practically devoured the food.

"It's okay I have some now?" he asked with trepidation.

Almost at the same time Loggam and Jenny replied, "Of course."

"Eat until your belly is nice and full," Jenny followed.

Tarzan grabbed that pizza with an ear-to-ear grin and gobbled it down as if he was in a race.

"Slow down, now. There's no hurry to finish," Loggam regarded. It was clear and troubling to see how hungry this child truly was.

Loggam and Jenny watched as this young little body ate five generous slices of pizza before bowing out.

"Wow, weren't you hungry. Ya know, Tarzan," Jenny started. "I don't know if you noticed, but we have many animals to tend to, and being you, Tarzan, we wondered if you'd be interested in staying with us for a while. Maybe helping with the animals? We have a spare room if you'd be interested?"

Loggam tried to read the little boy face. It seemed he was pleased with this idea.

"Hmm… One condition, I don't have to go to school or see those other boys again?"

Loggam and Jenny always listened carefully trying to figure out clues to where he was from. Now they wondered if he ran away from home because of school bullies.

"Well, for now, you can miss some school, but at some point, you will have to go back, and sooner rather than later. As far as the boys, are these boys at your school, you mean?"

"I don't wanna talk about it. I'd like to see my room, if that's okay?"

"Sure, follow us this way."

The room was at the end of the hall. It was an average-sized room with a twin bed for guests and pale-blue curtains. The room had a very quant ambiance about it.

"Wow, I've never seen a bedroom this big. Is it all for me, or do others sleep here too?"

"No one else. This is our guest room, and since you're our guest, this is where you'll sleep," Jenny said.

Though it was still a bit early, Tarzan was obviously tired after all of his travels and made even sleepier with his full belly. Jenny helped turn down the bed, and Tarzan jumped in and cuddled his small frame against the big quilt.

"If you need anything, we are here. You just call out. Tomorrow, we will introduce you to all our animals; it will be a fun time. I guess we probably need to grab you some proper clothes too," Jenny said as she tugged on the scrubs she gave him to wear. As she sat there with him and just talked about the animals they had, Tarzan's eyes slowly started to fade. He was trying to stay awake but quickly losing the battle.

Jenny decided it be best to take a few personal days from work. She would still go and visit her patients but this situation called for both her and Loggam. That morning, Loggam made his special pancakes and French toast for breakfast. They heard the pitter-patter of little feet against the floor before the "Tarzan yell" from the hallway. That got Fred's attention who wagged his tail and ran into the hallway to see where that noise came from. The hums of deep belly giggles came next from the hallway. Fred was licking Tarzan's face and causing him to have a giggle fit. It was the sweetest sound Jenny ever heard she thought. Finally, while following closely to Fred, Tarzan came out from the hallway and sniffed into the air.

"Something sure smells good," he said.

"That would be Loggam's special breakfast, which he prepared just for you," Jenny said.

With a quick knock at the door, the knob twisted, and Judith came in. "Well, whom do we have here?" she asked.

"Hey, Mom. We'd like you to meet our new friend, Tarzan."

"Hello there, Tarzan. It's nice to meet you. I'm Judith, Loggam's mom. I hear you're going to help me feed all the animals today, huh," Judith said.

"Yes, ma'am. I'd like that."

"Everyone come and eat," Loggam called out.

Once again, Tarzan waited briefly to take his food. When he finally trusted enough to fill his plate, he guzzled the food down fast again. Loggam and Jenny started to notice little traits about Tarzan. These were certainly things he intended to tell Detective Brandon about.

After breakfast was all cleaned up, the group went outside to feed and care for the animals. Tarzan was in his glory; he couldn't decide where he wanted to go first! All along, Fred stayed clung to his heels. Judith even made a comment that Fred found a new favorite! Tarzan fed the chickens, played with the goats, awed over the baby chicks.

And then he saw the horses. Tarzan stood as still as a statue staring at Duchess and Trigger, Loggam and Jenny's horses.

Judith walked over. "Are you okay?"

"I had only ever seen those on TV. I've never seen them in real life," Tarzan said.

"Well, why don't we go visit then? You know what horses' favorite treats are?"

"What?" he asked mystified.

Judith handed Tarzan a juicy big cherry-red apple. "They love apples. Watch me, all you do is lay your hand completely flat and place the apple on top. You'll feel their big horsy lips grab it right up!"

Tarzan followed Judith's instructions to the letter and fed the horse the apple.

"*Wow*! That was the coolest thing ever, I felt his fur itch my hand!" Tarzan's dimples had dimples he was smiling so hard.

The rest of the day was spent visiting and caring for each animal. As they went through the farm, Judith, Loggam, and Jenny enjoyed teaching Tarzan all about the animals and how to care for them.

Later that day, Detective Brandon stopped by just to meet Tarzan and inform Loggam that so far he still hasn't found anything on a missing child. Being they didn't want to startle Tarzan, they kept the visit very informal and friendly. Brandon even kept his badge discreet so he didn't alarm him. Brandon listened closely just as the other had in hopes of exhuming some pivotal information as to where he was from. Tarzan was certainly careful not to disclose anything they could go on.

That evening before dinner, Tarzan was exhausted after his fun-filled day. Spending the day outdoors had really made him sleepy. He sat on the couch petting Fred who sat pressed up against his lap. His eyes felt so heavy and Fred's fur became a nice resting spot for his head. After a few minutes, Tarzan was out like a light. Fred looked pretty content too.

"Hey, Ta—" Loggam started until he noticed he was fast asleep. He walked over, petted Fred on his head and laid a blanket across the two of them. Loggam couldn't help but feel a slight tug at his heart seeing this sweet boy sleeping so peacefully.

He walked outside to start grilling dinner and figured this was the perfect opportunity to talk to Brandon. "Well, what do you think Brandon?"

"It's clear wherever he is from, he doesn't want us knowing. I also noticed how he is about eating. Almost like he doesn't know when he's gonna eat again."

"Yeah, that was something we noticed too. All I know is he's safe and welcome here until he feels comfortable to tell us something."

"Now that your farm is up and running, when does Jenny want to open her petting zoo?"

"Soon, she's just waiting for medical clearance from both the families and the hospital to bring some of her patients here. She has many of them all excited and ready to go. We're hoping by next week we can bring the first set of them."

"Well, whatever I can do to help you just let me know. I will also keep my ears open for any info about Tarzan; something has got to pop up."

The next morning, Jenny was getting ready to go visit some of her patients at the hospital. As she finished putting on her makeup, she noticed Tarzan watching her from the doorway.

"Hi, sweetie. How are you this morning?"

"Good, hanging out with Fred. Are you going to the hospital?"

"Yes, I am."

"Oh, I thought so." Tarzan looked down and started drawing circles on the carpet with his toes.

"Is there something wrong?"

"I was kinda wondering, are some of the kids you see my age?"

"Well, yes. A few of them are your age actually."

"What is wrong with them that they have to live at the hospital?"

"Well, each of them is battling different types of the same illness. Some of them are doing really well on their medications and some of them still have some little ways to go before they will be better."

"Will they all get better?"

"Unfortunately, no, sweetheart. Sometimes our missions are shorter than others. Sometimes we go back home to God when we are still young. If that happens though, that means that their work here was all finished."

"All finished?" Tarzan questioned.

"We are all here to learn, grow and love. Sometimes we can complete what we need and go home faster than others. It's all in God's plan. We must be grateful for each day of good health and love with all we have. Do you understand that?"

"Yeah, I think I do. Is it okay if I come with you today?"

Jenny was surprised by Tarzan wanting to join her but happy to have him. "Of course, you can, I'm sure they'd love to meet you."

Jenny and Tarzan arrived at the hospital, as they walked in Jenny stopped and spoke with her many friends among the staff. They'd already been aware of her houseguest and were just happy to meet him. Each person who stopped to chat was more like family than a friend to Jenny. The hospital had become almost another home to her. As she entered her beloved pediatric ward, the kids walking around ran to her and cheered upon her arrival. Tarzan watched them and tried not to stare at their appearance. Jenny had already explained in the car ride their what this illness and the treatment caused so Tarzan wasn't surprised by what he saw.

Together, they walked from room to room as Jenny introduced Tarzan to each patient. They each giggled at his name, and it pleased him to cause them to smile. The final room they walked into was to an empty bed. "Hmm. I wonder where she went. Sara?"

"Over here," she said.

Tarzan turned to the voice and immediately felt goosebumps over his arms. *She's pretty*, Tarzan thought.

Sara had large deep-green eyes and dark-brown hair. Her pale skin shone against her hair. Tarzan never noticed a girl being pretty before; usually, girls were just annoying to him. Jenny introduced them as she did all the others, and Tarzan was a bit shyer. Not Sara though, she immediately started asking him many questions about his name and how he liked living with Loggam and Jenny and mostly about the farm and all the animals inhabiting it. Jenny took notice of the little friendship that seemed to be brewing between the two. She thought maybe even that Sara might gather more about Tarzan then even they had. Jenny had to go check on some work things and left the two kids chatting amongst themselves. Jenny went to the nurse's station, and she gathered all the authorization forms for the children who would be going to the farm. She couldn't wait to tell them they were in. For the children who wouldn't be able to join, she had already promised them the next best thing; a very special visit from Fred! Fred was registered specifically to go to the hospital and visit with the children.

Around lunchtime, Jenny had Tarzan and Sara go to the cafeteria for lunch with the other children. They all sat around getting to know one another, but it was plain to see that the conversation still did stay mainly between Sara and Tarzan. Jenny stood up and gathered the attention of the kids.

"Well, everyone, I've got good news. I have received all of your authorization letters, and how would you like to come to my farm this Friday?" An outpouring of happy cheers erupted from the room. Even Tarzan was hooting and hollering with cheerfulness.

When it was time to go home, Tarzan said goodbye to all the kids he met and a special goodbye to Sara. "I guess I will get to see you on Friday. If you want, I'll show you how to give the horses their favorite treats," he said with nervousness.

"I can't wait to see the horses. Oh yes, I'd really like that," she said.

Tarzan had a huge smile across his face; he was delighted with her excitement.

Now with the first group of kids coming, Loggam was rushing to try to get everything ready for them. He had special signs made that he'd stuck in the dirt in their necessary places. Some were about what the animals are and information about the animal. He also made sure he had a lot of feed for them and treats for the kids to give them. He had help with the finishing touches from some of the patrons of Red Fir State Park. They were regulars at the park and always came visit Loggam when they're visiting. Loggam had known the Deegans for many years. They had become family to him. Their two children, Casey and Pete Jr., were much older now and overjoyed to help Loggam set up his farm.

"Well, I think we have everything just about ready. How about we meet in an hour at Skully Lake for a nice campfire. I'll bring some BBQ," Loggam said.

"That sounds perfect, we will bring some snacks. See you in an hour," Pete said.

At Skully Lake Pete, Hannah, Casey, and Pete Jr. gathered around a roaring fire as Loggam, Jenny, Tarzan, and Fred walked up. Judy made her way over about a half an hour later. Loggam was happy to have all the extra mouths because he brought a lot of food. Even the Deegans brought food along. Tarzan was slowly becoming more and more comfortable among them. As the festivities continued, more campers joined the fun when they saw it was Loggam.

Guy Henderson and his son, Josh, walked up with fishing poles and tackle boxes in their hands.

"Guy!" Loggam yelled. "How're you doing, it's been a long time since you have been here, and Josh, you look like you've grown a whole foot since I saw you!"

"It certainly has been a while. We just came from doing some fishing and smelt your food cooking," Guy said.

"We followed our noses," Josh said while laughing.

Tarzan noticed Josh and Guy and tried to turn his head and walk in the opposite direction. Before he could make a clean getaway, Loggam called him over.

"Well, you boys are welcome to join us, we have plenty of food. Josh, Guy, I'd like you to meet Tarzan."

Guy studied Tarzan for a few moments, something about him rang familiarly, but Guy couldn't quite put his finger on it so both Guy and Josh smiled.

"Now that's a cool name. It's nice to meet you, Tarzan."

Tarzan shook the hands extended out to him. Josh was a bit more outgoing than Tarzan was so he led the conversation among them talking about fishing and the many different lures he had.

From across the crowd of friends, Jenny watched Tarzan with Josh. It was clear that he was more timid and shy. As time progressed, it seemed like Josh was pulling Tarzan out of his shell more and more. The two boys were becoming fast friends and that warmed Jennie's heart to see.

The next morning, everyone woke up bright and early. They all had a huge day ahead of them. This was the first day that the kids from the hospital would be coming to the farm, and Loggam, in his true fashion, wanted everything to be perfect for them. He had many helping hands later today from the Deegan family, his mother Judith, his friend Brandon and both Guy and Josh wanted to help out too. He was so lucky to be surrounded by such wonderful friends. Jenny would be heading to the hospital to prepare the children and make sure all their medical needs were 100 percent met before the field trip. Some of the other nurses would be coming along as well.

Everyone gathered at the farm awaiting their special guests. Loggam even purchased a cotton candy machine and popcorn maker. He hired a photographer so the kids could get pictures of the animals. As the bus pulled up, Tarzan started getting both nervous and excited. He couldn't wait to see Sara again.

When the doors opened and the first few kids came down the steps the expressions on their faces would have warmed even the Grinch's heart. As Sara stepped off the bus, she immediately looked through the people until her eyes met Tarzan's. She smiled big and walked right over to him.

"Hi, Tarzan. I'm finally here!"

Fred who was sitting beside Tarzan started nudging her hands to pet his head and that caused her to giggle.

"We're going to have so much fun today, Sara. I'll be your tour guide. I know all the animals personally," Tarzan said with pride.

All the kids gathered and were broken up into groups of three. Each group had both an adult and nurse to join them and take them around the farm. The Deegans set up a station for face painting and had many happy little girls. One wanted butterfly wings and another wanted sparkles and hearts. The day was going exactly how Jenny and Loggam dreamed it would; laughter filled their ears from all the children. Jenny had never seen the kids smile so much. Many of the children's parents also came along as well as bringing their other children. The little farm was just about filled to full capacity, but it was worth every moment. The parents all throughout the day greeted both Jenny and Loggam with such gratefulness and appreciation. It had been a long time for many of them to see their kids with such happiness and almost forget about being sick of not just for a couple of hours. The photographer snapped shot after shot, some were silly, and some were truly magnificent. For instance, she was able to catch the magic moment when one of the little girls riding the horse lowered her head against the horse's mane and closed her eyes and smiled. She caught the laughter when donkey's whiskers tickled the kid's hands.

Jenny eyes filled with tears as she took a step back and just looked all around her. This was her dream happening right before her very eyes. She watched as the children stared with awe at the horses. In no direction could she look that she didn't see the biggest, happiest smiles. The sounds of frequent laughter erupted all around her. The same kids she'd watch from day to day go through such tough treatments finally having a moment to just be the kids they are. She knew this was something they'd continue doing because every fiber of her being felt ignited with bliss. Jenny recalled better than most the sadness and fear that this illness caused. Not just for the person inflicted but the families of them as well. She also knew that laughter was truly the best medicine out there.

As the day drew closer to an end, Loggam and Jenny both admired Sara and Tarzan's blossoming friendship. It rang such familiarity for Loggam and Jenny as it reminded them of when they first met. Out of all the people Tarzan warmed up to, it was clear that Sara was the most.

With full bellies, faces full of paint, and ear-to-ear grins, it was time to leave. Loggam gathered all the kids and wanted to say a few words before they boarded the bus.

"It has been so wonderful having you all here today. We can't wait until you all come back and visit us all again really soon. Until then, Fred here will still be coming to visit you." Fred walked over to Loggam and stuck his snout under his hand to get Loggam to pet him. "See you all soon!"

Tarzan walked Sara over to the bus.

"Will you come and visit me at the hospital soon?"

"Yes, I'd like that. I'll come next time Jenny brings Freddy. I had a lot of fun with you today, Sara." Tarzan leaned in and hugged Sara gently. She kissed his cheek with a little giggle before boarding the bus.

Loggam and his friends started to clean up around the farm after the bus pulled away. He was so fortunate to have such good friends to lend a hand. When Josh and Tarzan went to brush down the horses, Guy took this opportunity to speak with Loggam. He asked Brandon to join them knowing this might be relevant information. The men walked over to a more discreet area so they wouldn't be interrupted.

"What's on your mind, Guy?" Loggam inquired.

"I don't know if this is something or not, but since yesterday, something has been bugging me. When Josh and I left Tennessee to come here, we stopped at the local diner for breakfast before we left. While there, we ran into a local cop friend of ours. He was telling us they were searching for a missing boy that ran away from a group home while they were out on a field trip. We told him we would keep an eye out, however, we were leaving for Alabama so we wouldn't be much help.

"From the diner, we pulled the RV into the gas station before hitting the highway, and I could have sworn right before the gas station, I had seen a young man who fit the description walking alongside the road. When I pulled up to the pump, a cop happened to be already in the store. Josh and I jumped out and went in, and of course, told him, but when we came out, he was gone. I don't even know if that was the boy or not, I assumed he was picked up—maybe he had been meeting someone. Ever since I met Tarzan yesterday, man, I would almost bet anything that was the same kid I had seen a picture of and walking alongside the street that day. I've been back and forth because what are the possibilities it's the same boy all the way from Tennessee?"

Loggam and Brandon looked at one another with deep suspicion. This was the clue they'd been looking for as to where Tarzan maybe came from.

"How would he have gotten all the way here?" Loggam said.

Brandon quickly fell into cop mode. "Well, this gives me a direction to search in. I'm going to run to the station and see if any APBs matching Tarzan's description is active in Tennessee. Thank you, Guy, for this information."

As Loggam finished up, his mind was reeling. His gut instincts told him this was the information they'd be searching for. Problem was, over the past few weeks, he'd grown to love Tarzan and no longer wanted to find out. But of course, he knew he had to do what was right. Somebody somewhere would be searching for him. He wasn't looking forward to telling Jenny that they might have a lead. He knew that she had grown especially attached to him too.

Later that night everyone was really sleepy. They'd had a long, wonderful day in the sunshine. Tarzan had fallen asleep on the couch with his head immersed in Fred's warm fur. Both Fred and Tarzan were snoring away. With a light knock on the door, Jenny and Loggam both quietly jumped up off the couch and went to the door. Brandon was there with a folder of paperwork. They led him into the dining room and spoke softly so they wouldn't be overheard.

"Well, I do not know how he got here, but that is definitely him," Brandon said as he opened the folder and put the papers across the table displaying his picture. "His real name is Turner Dern. He and his three-year-old younger sister were put into the foster system. They lived with their single mother, Molly, until she was killed in an accident. With no other family to speak of, the children were separated into foster care and group homes. I spoke with the group home he had been with the day he went missing, and they said he had been very unhappy being separated from his little sister and was having trouble dealing with the loss of his mom. They also said some of the other boys had been giving him trouble. They had just placed him in a foster home, but he never made it there. The day he went missing, they had been on a field trip at a local museum. He slipped away then and they've been looking for him ever since."

Both Jenny and Loggam were shocked and couldn't even find the words. They just fingered through the papers across the table in sadness.

"Poor kid. Not only to lose his mother but to then be separated from his sister and thrown into a new environment like that. Now I understand why he acted so timid and ate his food like it was a race every time," Jenny stated with tears coming down her face. As they spoke, Fred walked into the room and pawed at Brandon to say hello. Brandon pet his head as they continue speaking just above a whisper. Unbeknownst to them, Tarzan had awoken and was eavesdropping on their conversation. He couldn't make it all out because they spoke very low, but he knew the jig was up.

Brandon continued, "Of course, I had to alert them he was here, and we had him. Someone from the state will be driving up tomorrow to collect him. I am so sorry, guys."

Loggam grabbed Jenny's hand knowing the tears had started falling heavier now hearing those words. Loggam sat Jenny down into the chair and kneeled in front of her. He wiped away the tears falling from her checks.

"Jenny, it's not a secret we both have fallen in love with that boy. What do you say? Should we try to adopt him?"

Jenny's face lit up with hope and she hugged Loggam tight and nodded yes over and over again. Unfortunately, Tarzans eavesdropping only lasted until he overheard they were coming for him. With those words, he slowly went into his room, packed a book bag with clothes, and climbed out the window.

They decided they'd confront Tarzan with the information they just gathered. Once they gathered themselves and Jenny wiped away the wetness from her face they went into the living room where they left him. "Loggam, he's not in here. Maybe he went to bed?"

After seeing his room was empty, they searched the rest of the house.

"Oh no, what if he heard us and knew we found out?" Jenny said fearfully.

"Don't worry, he couldn't have gone far." With that, they all jumped into action. Brandon ran to his squad car and reported it over his radio. Loggam and Jenny grabbed flashlights and started on foot. The temperature had dropped a bit and it was a chilly night. They each went into different directions. Brandon used the spotlight in his squad car. No one knew these woods better than Loggam nor were they as good at tracking. In the darkness, it was a bit more difficult, but Loggam noticed some fresh tracks in the dirt and decided he'd follow those. They headed toward Red Fir State Park. He called out Tarzan's name as he followed the tracks. With a strong gust of wind, a shallow sound echoed into the night. Loggam stopped and shut his eyes and just listened. He found it sharpened his senses when he closed them. He heard the faint calls again and this time was able to get an idea of the direction.

He yelled back, "Tarzan!"

Again he heard it and made out the word "Help!" Loggam ran like someone set him on fire. His heart raced hearing his boy in trouble. He'd get to him if his life depended on it. The cries got louder and louder.

"I'm coming, Tarzan," he yelled back. Loggam stopped short to see the ground caved in. A large tree had fallen and caused a huge whole in the ground where the roots of the tree had been. During daylight, it would have been more obvious, but at night, you wouldn't know it until you fell in. Loggam jumped into the hole in the earth not caring that he didn't have gear to get back out. He had to make sure Tarzan wasn't badly hurt. Tarzan held his leg and cried out in pain. It was clear when he fell in, he had broken it. Loggam ran to him and checked him out. He had some cuts along his arms and was bleeding, but his leg was the biggest concern. Loggam quickly dialed Brandon's number knowing he was the closest with his car and could arrive even faster than an ambulance.

When Brandon arrived, Loggam and he created a plan to lift Tarzan out safely. They laid him across a makeshift stretcher and Loggam lifted it to Brandon, and Brandon pulled it up carefully until he was at ground level. Then Brandon grabbed Loggam's outstretched hand and helped him get out of the hole. After loading Tarzan into the car, Loggam called and updated Jenny while Brandon called into the radio about the fallen tree so no one else got hurt.

At the hospital, Tarzan was in the back being cared for when Jenny and Judith came bursting into the doors. Once they'd gotten the clearance to go see him, Jenny ran ahead of everyone and darted into his room. When she saw him lying in the bed with his leg all splinted she gently scooped his upper body into her arms and hugged him tight. She gently rocked him in her arms thanking God he was okay.

"You gave us a real scare. Why did you run away, sweetheart?"

Tarzan held her tightly back while quiet tears ran down his little cheek. "I...I heard you. I know you know who I am now. I know you're going to send me back to the group home. So I ran away."

"Well, I guess you didn't overhear the whole conversation then," Loggam said as he walked over and put his arm around Jenny. They both sat on the corner of the hospital bed.

"You're right, we do know who you are, son. But we also know something else." Loggam put his hand on Tarzan's shoulder and continued. "We know that we love you, and with your permission, we'd like to adopt you. How would you like to be our boy?"

Tarzan couldn't contain his tears and cried out in happiness. With a bit of a stutter, he said, "I want that, I've never wanted anything more." The three of them came together into a beautiful and warm embrace. Judith stood in the corner of the room and cried watching them all.

Tarzan had to stay in the hospital for a couple of days to monitor his bruising and his leg. Loggam and Jenny left Judith to watch over him so they could go to Tennessee and get the process for Tarzan's adoption going. Tarzan was happy to be at the hospital because he was able to spend a lot of time with Sara. She came to his room many times in the day to talk and play board games with him. Judith watched them both and felt a strong sense of nostalgia while doing so. She remembered like it was yesterday, a young blond Loggam and his friend Jenny. She lifted her book back over her eyes and just smiled while the two of them continued giggling about. Once Tarzan was given crutches, he asked to go to the hospital cafeteria; he was getting cabin fever stuck in his room. Sara and Tarzan both got large pretzels and sat down.

"I told you Tarzan," she said with a smirk.

"Huh?"

"I told you to believe in your dream. This is exactly what you told me you secretly dreamed of. My mom always told me, if your mind can believe it you can achieve it. That's how I know I'm going to be better one day soon."

Tarzan was praying with his whole heart that Sara would be better. "Ya know what Sara, I think I believe you," he said as he put his hand on hers.

"I do have one question, though." She wrinkled her nose and said, "How the heck did you get here from Tennessee?"

Tarzan's face grew mischievous as he started his tale. "Well, that's an interesting story. After I left the museum, I started walking not really sure where I was going. I just knew I had to get away from those mean boys. I wanted to find my little sister Katie, but I didn't have a clue where to start. So after a while of walking, I had heard police sirens in the distance, and I knew I had to get off the main road before I was spotted. I had seen a gas station ahead and I was really thirsty. So I made a run for it, I almost ran smack into an RV because I wasn't paying attention. When I walked out of the gas station with my yoo-hoo, I saw a man and his kid running into the gas station pretty quickly. I knew he probably spotted me on the street too. That's when I had the big idea... I climbed into their camper when they were in the store, and I found a crawl space with lots of large comforters in it. I climbed in under them and stayed put. A few times they stopped, I listened and contemplated getting out. That was before I heard them talking about the fishing they were going to do in Alabama. I decided I could make it, and I waited until I was sure they arrived and were both out before I made my escape. I grabbed a jacket I saw and ran into the woods. I was lost in what I now know is Red Fir State Park for a few days before Loggam found me. I was really scared to be honest, and starving."

Sara's eyes were wide throughout his story. "I can't believe you hid in a crawl space under blankets for that many hours. Was the group home really that bad?"

"Well, maybe not for some, but for me it was horrible. Ya see, I was the smallest guy and the other guys pushed me around. They never left any food for me, and even when I was handed my one plate, one of them would steal it when no one was looking. The worst part of all was I missed my mom and sister." Tarzan's face grew saddened and a tear slipped down his cheek. Sara didn't want to pry but she was curious what happened to her.

Before she couldn't ask, Tarzan continued on. "We were the three musketeers; myself, my mom, and my little sister Katie. I had never met my dad, my mom used to tell me he had a job in heaven that took him away from us. We used to do everything together. My favorite was when she'd take us sleigh riding in the winter. We didn't get snow too often, but boy, we had fun when we did. Once she even took us to Dollywood. It was one of the best days I ever had. One day I was waiting for her to pick me up from school, and she was really late. After a while, the teacher brought me back into the school and made some phone calls. Next thing I know, a woman and a police officer showed up and brought me to what they call a foster family. It was there they told me my mommy had a car accident and wasn't coming back. I tried to stay strong for my little sister, but then her and I were separated. I was placed from one foster home to the next. Some of them were really nice people, but in the end, I went to the group home."

Sara could see the deep pain in Tarzan, as he had spoken his voice cracked and many tears were shed. "I'm so sorry Tarzan." Sara moved her chair close to Tarzan and leaned over to hug him. They held one another in a long embrace. Like a needle to thread, it was clear these two children found solace and contentment among one another.

It had been about a week Loggam and Jenny had been gone working hard to get all their adoptions ducks in a row. They had hoped to be back before Tarzan was released but unfortunately unable to do so. Tarzan was happy to stay with Judith until they returned. Each day Judith and Tarzan got to know one another more and more. Judith adored being a grandma. They baked cookies together, made crafts, watched movies, and he even was teaching her how to play video games. After about another week had passed, Loggam and Jenny were set to arrive back the next day. Tarzan couldn't wait to see them. Luckily, he had Fred with him the whole time, which did ease him missing them.

Judith and Tarzan prepared for their arrival the night before making all sorts of cookies. He couldn't wait to hear what happened, and he prayed he would be able to stay with them. After he took his bath and washed up for bed, Judith tucked him in.

"It's going to be okay, sweetheart, you'll see. When my boy sets his mind to something, he always achieves it." She kissed him on his cheek and started leaving the room.

"I love you, Grandma," Judith's heart melted upon hearing those words for the first time. It just about took her breath away. She walked back over and gently caressed his cheek.

"I love you too, sweetheart."

Loggam and Jenny arrived early in the morning. They had a surprise for Tarzan, and they were both glad he was asleep. Judith woke up and helped them prepare. Stealthily, Loggam tiptoed into Tarzan's room and gently sat on the corner of the bed. When Tarzan opened his eyes he was shocked to see Loggam.

"You are officially our son!" Tarzan jumped out of bed the best he could with his leg still healing and dove into Loggam's awaiting arms. While in the hug, Tarzan looked around the room to see balloons, so many balloons.

"Look at all these balloons!"

"We have a few more surprises for you, buddy. Come on!" Loggam grabbed Tarzan's hand and they went out to the living room where Jenny was standing. Tarzan ran into her arms and she wept as she embraced her son. Something she thought she'd never be able to have.

From across the room, suddenly, a loud "Brother!" roared out. Tarzan's body spun just in time for his little sister Katie to jump into his arms. He did all he could to contain himself. He hadn't seen her in such a long time; he must be dreaming he thought. This was the biggest wish he held within his heart. He ran his fingers over her soft blond tendrils.

"Katie, oh, Katie. I have missed you. I am never letting you go again. Does this mean she's staying too?" He asked with excitement and trepidation.

"Yes, we had taken a bit longer than we thought because we were on a quest to find and adopt her too."

Together, the siblings just stayed glued together weeping with merriment. Loggam and Jenny couldn't help but cry watching the two of them reunite. It was one of the most beautiful moments they'd ever been lucky enough to create. They joined them into a hug and the four of them held one another. Nothing else seemed to matter in this moment.

This. This was it, Loggam thought. His sweet mother standing affectionately near, his remarkable wife and now his two beautiful children. This was life. This was happiness.

Epilogue

After several months had passed, Tarzan and Katie transitioned beautifully into their new lives. The adoption was finally successful for both of the children. The only request being from Tarzan to keep his new name. Both Loggam and Jenny were happy to concede to that, considering they'd only known his as Tarzan anyhow. Both Jenny and Loggam were born to be parents. They loved spending every moment with the kids. Judith was in her grandma bliss and spent every second she could spoil her new grandchildren.

The Maggel farm had grown almost double in the past months. Jenny had decided she wanted to open their farm to abandoned animals or any animals in need. It was such a large undertaking that the Maggels had to purchase more property and hire builders this time to have the adequate space for them. It had taken off so well that even from other states, animals were being shipped in. After some time, the state even got involved and provided services and funding to help it grow. From all over the country, people would come to visit all the animals and pay homage to what the Maggels had accomplished. Many would volunteer either financially or bringing along goods for the animals. In such a short amount of time, a small idea became a dream fulfilled. So many members of the community volunteered their time.

Jenny continued to bring her patients from the hospital to visit. They found out shortly after the first ever visit that many of the kids had better test results after their day on the farm. It was clear that spending time away from the hospital's surroundings did them beyond good. They regularly called their outings "mental health" days. Jenny was in the process of getting more hospitals in the area on board.

One day, Loggam woke Tarzan up just as the sun was rising into the dark-blue sky. "Shh," he mouthed. "Come with me."

The two quietly left the house with Tarzan still in his Star Wars pajamas. Loggam was carrying something Tarzan couldn't quite make out. "I'm going to teach you something, Tarzan, that means more then you realize. As you get older, you'll understand why this matters more." With that, Loggam reached into the container in his hand and grabbed a heaping load of coins and tossed them throughout the walking path. Tarzan's mouth opened wide.

"It was you, Pa? I found all those coins I'm collecting in my room. Why do you throw your money away?"

"Well, son, do you recall the first time you found all that loose change?"

"Well, sure I do. I felt really lucky. Almost like I won something."

Loggam kneeled down to be at eye level with Tarzan. "When life gives you blessings, the most important thing you can do with that is give blessings to someone else. When we show that kindness towards others, not only does it come back to you, but it also feels really good. Go one and grab a huge handful, son."

Tarzan reached in deep as change slipped through his little fingers.

"Now, toss it!"

Tarzan threw the change up into the air and giggled as it rained down into the dirt.

"Now, the key is, you don't tell anyone you've done this. Remember the golden rule, any chance you have to help others is a good use of your time."

Tarzan looked deep in his dad's eyes and clung to every word. "Can I toss more?"

"Sure, you can. How about you join me on my walks, and we can always do this together?"

"I'd love that, Dad."

Together, father and son walked off into the morning light, scattering a little joy along their journey.

About the Author

Valerie grew up in a quaint rural community in Hudson Valley, New York, where she was surrounded by cousins, aunts, uncles, and her grandparents. She spent most of her days in imaginative play alongside her brother and cousins. Inspired by her wonderful grandfather, Fred, who was a poet, Valerie always had a penchant for writing. If you can't find Valerie among her fur babies, you will find her wrapped up in a cozy blanket with hot cocoa and a book. The smell of a good book and the feel of the pages against her fingertips are just some of her favorite companions. Having the ability to escape through the written word, it was only natural that she too could create that world for others. Although an avid reader of many genres, it was Valerie's warm and nurturing upbringing that moved her to write the story in this book. In addition to writing, Valerie is a lover of animals. She and her husband, Ben, have a dog and two cats, which keep them entertained with their adorable antics. Aside from writing, she also has a wood crafting business with her husband, which is another of Valerie's creative passions.

CPSIA information can be obtained
at www.ICGtesting.com
Printed in the USA
LVHW042255120520
655430LV00006B/424

9 781645 842590